WAKE UP AND ROAR

Volume 1

satsang with H.W.L. Poonja

Wake Up and Roar
Volume 1

ISBN 0-9632194-1-3
Library of Congress Catalog Card Number 92-80404

© 1992 by Pacific Center Publishing
P.O. Box 818
Kula, Maui, Hawaii 96790
(808) 878-3000

Printed on acid-free recycled paper.

Contents

Foreword

On January 1, 1990, I left my life behind and went on a search for enlightenment. My wife and friends thought I was mad. Since I was nearly forty-three years old, they chalked it up to a mid-life crisis.

At the time of my leaving, I had no idea where I was going or what I would find. Nor did I have any choice in the matter. I was pulled like an iron filing to a magnet.

Since I was not a beginner on the path, I had certain criteria for my search. I was looking for the final cutting of the egoic mind. I told my wife, "I want to wake up in the non-dual reality."

I was part of the generation that had discovered psychedelics twenty-five years earlier. I had experimented widely with LSD and other hallucinogens in my search for freedom. As a result of these experiences, I considered myself relatively awake as an enlightened soul. LSD had shown me that this "waking reality" is a dream, and I had directly experienced myself as self-conscious immortality. Still, this was not enough. The egoic suffering continued. In fact, the ego claimed the realizations as its own.

In the civil rights and anti-war movements of the 1960's, I was given ample opportunity to give my life to Life. By testing the courage of my convictions and being willing to die to stop

the suffering of the world, I discovered myself to be a servant
of Mother Earth. I therefore thought that "I" had to do something. And this something always eventually led to suffering.

In the wake of the genuine opening that many members of
my generation experienced with psychedelics came the gurus.
When the first wave of gurus came to America I was very interested. In 1974 and 1975, I sat with Swami Muktananda,
and enjoyed reading Rajaneesh and Da Free John. I followed
Ram Dass' adventures with Neem Karoli Baba and his other
teachers.

While with Muktananda I very much enjoyed the bhakti
and the shakti. I had not believed it possible for a non-pyche-
delically induced state to be as powerful as LSD. I discovered
differently. However, I was not particularly drawn to the ashram life. I knew about all the public Hindu gurus, from Sai
Baba to Maharaji, but when I looked at the followers and the
ashrams, my conclusion was that instead of enlightenment
what was created were devotees. I was looking for enlightenment and someone who could directly transmit it. As great
and enjoyable as the states of shakti were, they did not lead to
full Self-realization, at least not for me or anyone else I had
known.

In the early days of LSD, reading Carlos Castenada, Gurd-
jieff's works, and the *Tibetan Book of the Dead*, I became
attracted to Tibetan Buddhism. In 1976 I shared the Evans-
Wentz books of Tibetan Buddhism with my future wife and
expressed a desire to find the true holders of this lineage. In
1978, they found us. In that year Kalu Rinpoche, meditation
master of the Kagyu lineage, came to our small town in California and appointed me the head of his Dharma Center. We
did pujas and prostrations and learned to chant in Tibetan. We
helped arrange the Karmapa's visit to San Francisco and his

Black Hat Ceremony. Ultimately, it was not satisfying. No one that I could see was getting enlightened.

In the early 1980's I went to Japan. I met the oldest living Zen master at the time; I called him *O'ji isan*. Through our heart connection he presented me with a Zen teaching fan. I also did dharma combat in Saikoji Monastery. I experienced a deep spontaneous awakening, *kensho*, in the presence of the head of the monastery. It was celebrated by the entire monastery. After my kensho was announced we spent the night drinking beer and singing songs. We were even permitted to sleep in until 6:00 the next morning.

And still the next morning the same mind was present. I was not satisfied.

I then investigated vipassana meditation. This endless mental observation of objects seemed useful as a beginning stage, but I was hungry for what lay beyond the seer and the object of observation.

I also met and worked with my uncle Henry, medicine pipe holder of the Arapaho (the Blue Sky People). Uncle is pure essence with a heart as big as the sky. I love Uncle and everything he stands for and his work in this world. But I desired something more.

Several years later, I was initiated and adopted into a Gnauer Sufi clan. It was a profound, mystical experience. I was tested and had to defend our circle in dangerous circumstances on the coast of Morocco. Layeshay, the head of the clan and a descendent of palace slaves, took me into his heart and adopted me like a son. I love him and cherish the time we spent together.

By the winter of 1989, I was considered "a success." I was happily married to my best friend and lover for the past 13 years. I was a published author and workshop leader teaching spiritual psychology. I had a successful private practice in

San Francisco, a wonderful home in Marin County, and I traveled around the world leading workshops. Working with the Enneagram of Character Fixation, I had developed a new map of the psyche that integrated the Tibetan Buddhist model with Western psychology and the Sufi work with essence.

When this model was complete, I looked inside and saw what was lacking in my own development. I was still not fully awake. I was still subtly creating suffering in my life and in the lives of others. I was still acting out of ego fixation at least part of the time.

When I was pulled to India and preparing for my journey, I examined everything in my life. I was willing to give up everything except my love for my wife. I had several wrenching days, crying and sobbing at the thought of having to leave her. I later discovered, at the feet of my Master, that all I had to give up was the suffering! Love never needs to be given up.

When I left for India, I had no idea where I was going. My criteria was to find someone fully awake who could transmit this to me. If I could find no one awake at this level, I wanted to at least find some Sufis who knew the enneagram.

I landed in Delhi on January 5, 1990. My plan was to find enlightened Sufis, perhaps in the frontier region of Pakistan, or journey to Sikkim to find a Tibetan Lama from whom I had received a non-verbal transmission a few years earlier.

My first night in Delhi I went to the old Muslim neighborhood, Nizamuddhin, which I learned about from my hotel-keeper. I visited the shrine of Nizamuddhin, a 15th-century Sufi saint, and prayed for guidance and full awakening. I then went to dinner at Karim's, a local Muslim restaurant. As I waited to order, I watched another man come in and sit down with his back to me at a nearby table. Instead of taking my order first, the waiter approached the other customer. I fumed a bit at this slight. When the waiter approached my table to take my order, the other customer turned around and said, "I will pay for whatever he wants." He then asked if he might join me.

He was a government minister in town just for the day. His sister wrote books about the Sufis, and he claimed to know the special ones. He was flying out the next day, but would give me a list of the special Sufis he knew. When he returned to his home in Lucknow he would give me more names. He arranged for my introduction to the head of the Naqsbandi Sufis in old Delhi and had me taken back to my hotel in his chauffeur-driven government car.

I spent the next two weeks visiting the Sufi saints of the Naqsbandi and other sects. I was disappointed wherever I went. During that time I also received my visa for Pakistan and Sikkim and made arrangements to fly into Lahore.

Before leaving for Pakistan, I decided to visit my new friend, the government minister, at his home in Lucknow, where he had promised to give me more names. I also knew there was another teacher in Lucknow. I had met one of his students in California, and had asked the student for his teacher's address before leaving California, but my request had been denied. At this point I did not have the teacher's name or address.

When I arrived in Lucknow I called my wife to see if she could get the name and address of this other teacher. She could only give me his name: *Poonja*. I felt a strong pull to find him but had no idea how to begin.

I went up to the roof of my hotel (the Carlton, which was an old palace) and once again called for help. I looked up in the sky and saw a sign. I had never seen anything like it before. A red square and a black one dancing together. I then knew that this was where Poonja lived. (A week later Papaji showed me Indian kite flyers and I recognized what I had seen.)

I came down from the roof and found a telephone book. The page of *p*'s had been torn out. I found another phone book and there was the address of a *Poonja*. On inquiry, I found it was exactly where the kites had shown me it would be.

On January 19, 1990, my forty-third birthday, I walked through the back streets of the Narhi market, an old neighborhood of Lucknow. After being guided by several helpful neighbors I was shown to a small door in a row of attached houses. I knocked on the door. A man answered, and with a big smile said, "Yes, he is upstairs. He is waiting for you."

I went up the stairs of a tiny courtyard and into a small bedroom. He was sitting on his bed. "Come in, come in," he greeted me. The room was big enough for his bed and a chair. He asked me to sit on the bed with him.

"Why did you come?" he asked.

"I am really ready to wake up," I said. He laughed and laughed and we embraced. In that moment there was no question. I had met my Master. I knew without a trace of doubt that I was looking at my own Self.

"You know," he said, "a boy recently came here from Australia. He had a burning question. The question grabbed him and he jumped on a plane to come here with only the clothes he was wearing. It was wintertime and he only had a T-shirt and his pants. I loaned him my sweater and other warm clothes. But he had to have an answer to his question." He paused and looked at me. "He wanted to know, 'Is it my will that manifests the universe?' " As he told me this, Sri Poonjaji gave no hint at the answer. He just looked at me.

For the first time in my life I had been posed with a spiritual question for which I had no ready answer. I knew that I "knew" theoretically, but not directly. As he looked at me, I could say nothing at all. In that moment my mind stopped, and all my "knowing" temporarily disappeared. I had met my match.

Within a few days I started writing this book. The original title was *With a Living Zen Master.*

I spent the next four or five days alone with Sri Poonjaji. I asked if I could call him *Baba.* He laughed and said he didn't mind. Then I noticed that his grandchildren called him *Papaji,* and soon I did also. Each day was a timeless eternity of bliss. After two days I gave him my passport, tickets, and money. I told him I no longer cared about enlightenment. I only wanted to sleep outside his door and care for him. He laughed and playfully slapped me.

We went on daily walks together. He would take me to see the local sights and taste the local food. Each time we stopped to buy something, either from a street vendor or a small shop, he always paid.

In the evenings we had dinner together, prepared by his grandchildren, and then we went up to his room where he read and answered his mail. During this time with the Master and his son Surendra we would discuss the day's *satsang.* * I read early passages of this book to Papaji, which he enjoyed and encouraged.

One evening it dawned on me what I was to give up. Not just this life or this world, but the entire universe!

"None of it ever existed," he said with a smile.

"Papaji," I said, "although I have known that this life was a dream, I took Bodhisattva vows. I promised to come back."

"Oh my God!" he said, with mock horror on his face. "It is

---

* *satsang* - association with Truth

a good thing that I found you or you would have brought me back with you!"

Eventually he said that others were waiting to come and see him. I cried and said, "No, don't let them. I am jealous." Again, he laughed and slapped me.

"You sit and watch," he said.

And what I saw was a miracle. I watched people come in and, in the space of weeks, get enlightened and leave. I had thought he was a Zen master. Yet, when a bhakta of Anandamaya Ma came, he spoke as a Hindu. He spoke to the vipassana practitioners of the teachings of the Buddha. He spoke to the Christians of the inner meaning of the teachings of Jesus. When someone mentioned Sufis, he told stories of Kabir.

His speaking was no different than the depth of silence that radiated from him. When I asked him about cutting the mind, he told me to just be quiet. I did, and the mind stopped. What a miracle! I had never been with a spiritual teacher who had even allowed the possibility of the mind stopping. Here was a Master by whose grace the mind effortlessly stopped for dozens of people.

Lao Tzu (in the Taoist classic *The Tao Teh Ching)*, the Chan master Hui Neng, and the great Zen master Huang Po all speak and write from "no-mind." The possibility of no-mind being directly transmitted to all who want it was beyond my wildest dreams. What my Master directly showed me is that the experience of living in no-mind is the gateway to the bliss of Self-recognition.

• • •

I watched a constant flow of people from all over the world pass through Papaji's living room. Now the satsangs had grown too large for his bedroom, and six to ten of us managed to fit in the small living room. I watched people learn to effortlessly drop the mind and the idea of a personal ego, and thereby discover what has always been true and present. One by one people identified themselves as "Emptiness," "Silence," "Love."

I also noticed an incredible rudeness. Most people had no idea what they were walking into. Some came on their way to ride the elephants in Rajasthan, others came for a few days because they were in the area. Papaji invited everyone into his home and treated all as guests. He served tea and cookies and fruit, he took people for walks and bought them food. And many missed this extraordinary opportunity entirely. They saw a kind old man who appeared to be filled with love. Some called him *Poonja,* without even the courtesy of adding a *ji.* (As if they were calling someone "Hey, Smith" at home.) Some would sit in his living room and not introduce themselves. And others, unaware of what they were getting into, fell into his grace and were enlightened.

Papaji would take a daily walk and satsang would happen while strolling in the street or sitting under a tree. He would take us into the middle of the marketplace to discover that inner silence and darshan need nothing externally. He would take everyone for sweets in the market or to eat at his favorite street vendors.

• • •

Poonjaji says that a true teacher asks absolutely nothing from his students. He is a true teacher. Because he asked nothing, many gave nothing, not even politeness. This never stopped him from giving everything. For those with eyes to see, here was the rarest event in this world: the opportunity to spend time in the presence of a living saint, a true Buddha, who was speaking pure truth and passing on the flame of enlightenment and freedom to all who entered his door.

It amazed me that on our walks some people would wander off in clusters, chatting about inconsequentials. They acted as if this rarest of all events was no big deal. They were in the presence of a true living Master and took it for granted. Others were so drawn to the living love that they could not take their eyes off him. They drank deeply and were given everything! Nothing was ever asked in return.

Papaji did not let me stay with him, or change anything whatsoever in my life. By the end of February I had to leave. I told him I would return with my wife to see him, which made him very happy. I told him my wife was a goddess and that, though she started as my student, for the past several years she had been my teacher.

Before my leaving India, he wanted to show me the Ganga.* (He loved the Ganga and many years earlier, at the Kumbha Mela, the spirit of the Ganga had taken darshan from him. After he had retired and his children were married, his obligations were complete, and he had lived in a cave at the banks of the Ganga.)

We took a second class sleeper from Lucknow to Hardwar. We slept with strangers snoring in the same curtained compartment. The train arrived in Hardwar at 5:00 a.m. Papaji arose at 4:00 to make sure we were all up and ready. (Did I mention that at the time he was eighty years old?) We sat in the station from 5:00 until 7:00 so we wouldn't disturb anyone at the place where he rents his room.

Many people have offered him houses and ashrams all over the world, yet he has always refused. "It is repugnant to me to own a piece of Mother Earth," he says. "Once I was visiting a

---

* the river Ganges

tea plantation in the south. After the manager finished show-
ing me around, I found a wonderful Mandarin orange tree. I
said to the tree, 'Oh, what a wonderful mother you are with all
of your babies.' I have never picked a fruit or flower in my life.
I just stood there admiring the tree, and in that moment she
dropped a dozen oranges at my feet. Mother Earth takes very
good care of me."

As we sat in the train station waiting for dawn, he said,
"Once I arrived in Delhi at 2:oo in the morning. I slept outside my friend's door until the family awoke at 6:oo. If I had
an ashram, they would never permit me this freedom."

I asked if it were possible to live in an enlightened community. He said, "Let the thieves live together, and let the enlightened few spread out through the world."

December 15, 1991

This book is based on tape-recorded satsangs that occurred in Lucknow and Hardwar, India, between January 1990 and April 1991. The satsangs, which were open to everyone, took place in the home of Sri H.W.L. Poonja, a fully Self-realized Sat Guru. The voices and questions of the various participants are presented here as one voice.

Sri Poonjaji was born October 13, 1910, in the western part of the Punjab. He experienced his first *samadhi** at the age of nine. He met his master, Bhagavan Ramana Maharshi, in 1944. He continued to work and support many members of his extended family until his retirement in 1966.

After living on the banks of the Ganga and traveling the world, he now resides in Lucknow, India. Since seekers now number in the hundreds, satsang has outgrown his home and is happening in a larger house in his neighborhood.

April 1992

* *samadhi* - state of bliss

...y of Freedom

...here is a river of thought-waves. Everyone is being washed downstream. Everyone is clinging to these thoughts and being washed away.

Just give rise to the single thought, "I want to be free." This thought will rarely come out of the entire population. The entire population of the planet is moving downstream. They are not destined to give rise to the thought, "I want to be enlightened in this very span of time."

So I call this thought of freedom going against the stream and towards the source. It does not require any effort to give rise to this thought. The thought "I want to be free" is itself free. This thought will take you to freedom. It is the most rare thought. Out of the entire population of 6 billion, only a handful give rise to this thought.

Master, I have been with you for four days now, and I am still not enlightened.

(laughing) Yes, I am surprised, a smart boy like you.

What should I do?

Let me tell you what my teacher told me. Just be quiet.

This quiet does not involve talking or not talking. It does not involve any doing whatsoever. Just let the mind fall into silence. This is enough.

Now wait. I can't believe what you just said to him. I've been trained to think that it takes years and years of practice and lifetimes of training and hard work to reach liberation. Now you say it's simply a switch on the wall, a change of perception. Is that correct?

You need not switch on or off. For the sun to shine do you switch it on?

No.

Just like this. This light is always there. No switches at all. The sun has no switches. You turn your face away and you call it night. Sun has no night and no day. You are that sun. This is your own light and you are that. You don't need any switches. The switches are limitations. You have fixed these limitations yourself. Nature has not fixed any switches.

"I want this, I want that. I dislike this, I like that." If you remove this switch of like and dislike, how will you feel? Instantly you will be free. Likes and dislikes keep you in bondage and suffering.

There are no walls for the switches either. Walls are imaginary only, like walls between countries. You have constructed this wall between you and something else. You have to break this which does not exist.

The frontier you have created is the suffering. You have to demolish it by yourself. Nobody will help you.

What do you mean, "nobody will help you"?

The Self has to help the Self; nobody else can help. Who else will drop this wall? You have to help yourself. Find out, is it possible to be out of the Self, ever?

First say, "I want help." Then discover who needs help. Self is not suffering. Self is not in bondage. Self is ever free.

So you are saying it is the mind clinging to the wall that is suffering?

Yes. Who has created separation? Mind has created separation, and no mind will remove this separation. The separation doesn't exist. Even to say "I am separate" is a joke.

It is only when there is a need for understanding that there is something to be understood. Once some of Krishnamurti's students came here to see me. They said there is only one difference between our teachings. They said, "Krishnamurti removes concepts from the vessel and Poonjaji breaks the vessel altogether." *(laughs)*

So allow yourself some time, a couple of moments. And in those moments there should be no trespassing. Make available a few seconds and during this span nobody should trespass. I think you could well afford to be available for a few moments. You have spent all your life for others, and not even a minute for your Self.

Everyone possesses you. When you are born, your parents say you are "my son." Go to school next and you're "my student." Then marry and you're "my husband." Have children and you're "my father." Remove these possessions. Let no one possess you. Reject everything and see what happens.

You have to devote some time for your Self, either now or

some other lifetime. You have to reach your home. There is no escape. You have to return home, either now or tomorrow. You must decide if you want to play more. It doesn't matter. In the end, it doesn't matter.

You think it is taking time. It is no time that you are spending because you are already free; it is only your illusion that you are not. You have to allow time, once and for all, if you want to be happy. The moment you declare "I AM FREE!"—standing on the mountaintop of your toes, arms up—Eureka! There is the happy moment. Very happy moment.

• • •

What prevents you from freedom? What is the impediment?

That I often have lots of thoughts and it is very difficult to get rid of them.

What kind of thoughts do you have? Do you give rise to the thought of freedom?

Yes.

Hold onto this thought of freedom. Do you see any other thoughts simultaneously rising up?

No.

Mind can hold onto only one thought at a time.

I understand.

Tell which other thoughts replace this thought of freedom. Voluntarily bring another thought to replace this. Another thought that you like best. Do it . . . do it!

I don't want to reject this thought.

Very good. Very nice. When you like this thought, where will this thought take you? Where will other thoughts be? Where is freedom? How many kilometers away from you?

I don't think it is far away from me.

If it is not far from you, then how much time is needed for you to arrive here? How much time to be as you are? It is here and now. How much time to be here and now?

As little as possible.

Let us agree, as little as possible. Should we call it this moment? This instant? The least possible time. This instant is the time. Now look at this moment, the least time. Look into this instant, if it is not far away. Jump into it right now.

How?

Now!

(much laughter)

Now, what is the thought now?

None. Only this now.

No thoughts troubling you now?

Only that I am looking for thoughts.

Yes, yes. Keep on looking for thoughts. Do you understand what you are saying?

Yes.

If you don't look for a thought, the thoughts will look for you. If you don't look, all the thoughts will attack you. Try. If you look for a thought, do you catch it?

They have disappeared.

Then when the thoughts have disappeared, who are you?

(silence)

This is the best answer you can give me. Stay as such. If you step out of the silence, there is trouble. You don't need anything. Eternity is here. Happiness is here. No death can enter this silence. No trouble can enter here. Step out and there is *samsara*. Endless cycle of birth and death. No thought, no concept can enter here. All desires are met here in emptiness. You walk out chasing after desires and they are never fulfilled.

• • •

All my life, even as a little boy, the desire for freedom has been stronger than all other desires. It doesn't really seem to be a desire; it's more like a longing. This desire seems to pull me back while the

*other desires seem to pull me out. This desire for freedom myster-
iously seems to stay, where the other desires come and go and
change with my thoughts. The desire for freedom is always there,
burning. It seems to be deeper than the mind. Is this true?*

This is the most intense desire. All other desires are on the
surface. They rise and fall, you see. The desire for freedom is
intense and you must respond to it. When you respond, this
desire will bring you back home. It will continue to trouble
you if it is not fulfilled in this life span.

This desire must be fulfilled, whether you like it or not.
That is why you come here. What a farce! This desire follows
you wherever you go, in whichever incarnation you take. It
will not leave you. How did it push you here? You left your job
and your business; why did you have to come here? Just consider it. You must return home! How long can you stay at the
market?

*It seems the only response to the desire is to look within to
where the mind originates. To go to the place where thoughts arise
and stay with it. That is the response, isn't it?*

Yes. You will unceasingly scan the mind. Unceasingly. And
you will know who you are.

Purification

When I think of the notion of purification it seems absolutely ridiculous. I wonder if you would speak about the value of purification. Many teachers tell their students to do more purification so that their realization is more powerful.

First of all, to purify yourself there must be some dust inside the teacher's mind and he wants someone to wipe it out. There is, in truth, no dust at all. It is a waste of time to purify what is not dusty. From where has the dust accumulated? And where will you move this dust to; where will you throw it? With which broomstick will you do it? If you look, there is no place for dust to alight. Better to dust out the concept of purification. You are that emptiness itself. Where can dust alight?

Who Are You?

A new visitor was asked this question:

Who are you? I'll give you five minutes because you are Indian. These others may think I treat you better because you are an Indian and they are all foreigners. So I will. I will give you five minutes for this question.

Five minutes! I have been working on this question for 2½ years!

You are right. Five minutes is too long, but you are a guest. I want to treat you well.

Look, how far is it from Kanpur, where you came from, to here?

About 90 kilometers, about three hours.

Three hours. Now why does it take three hours?

Because of the distance.

Very good, very good. So where is the *I* that is asking the question? And where is the *I* in "Who am I?" I gave you five

minutes to be polite. But if there is no space—no distance—
your answer should take no time!

• • •

*I was very touched yesterday when you spoke of obedience.
Living obedience every second, obedience to that every second.*

Yes.

Obedience implies a duality, doesn't it?

It is your own Self. Where is the duality?

Only Self.

You love your Self. Is it not obedience?

The river merging, the river discharging into the sea—is it
not obedience? Externally, you can call it obedience, going
back to meet herself. You can call it obedience, or you can call
it return to the source, according to your temperament. And
the ocean is happy to receive you.

If obedience is given to anyone else then you call it duality.
But where is duality? You have two hands, two feet, ten
fingers, a nose . . . how many parts to this body, but when you
say "I," is it duality?

When you see your face in the mirror, are there two persons? When you see truth you know there has never been
duality. Right from the beginning until the end of the universe.

*I was thinking of the Self creating multiplicity for its own
enjoyment.*

When you cross the ocean you will see the emptiness of unity. When you dream you see many different people, of many different ages, and you see mountains that are millions of years old and different stars or whatever. And when you are awake, was what you saw in the dream unity or multiplicity?

A dream within the unity.

When you wake up, unity also goes. Duality goes also. So when you wake up from this waking sleep you return to emptiness. Whenever we see objects we are dreaming. And when we are dreaming, this means we are also sleeping. So you have to wake up with a shout: "I want to be free!" With this shout you will wake up and everything goes. Otherwise you will be reborn again and again in endless cycles of *kalpas*.

• • •

Is enlightenment or Self-realization just an awareness, a self-evident awareness of Being?

Yes, it is awareness. Total awareness or Being, same thing. No difference. Total awareness. Everything is there. And you are that awareness.

I have this awareness. Yet, as everybody knows, your realization is much deeper than mine. What is the difference?

You make a difference. Otherwise, there is no difference.

If I were to sit there, where you are, after one week nobody would come here anymore.

You can try. Come here. *(everyone laughs)* When I asked the difference, my master removed my difference and I accepted it.

Maybe this is the point. I do not accept enough. But I have it.

Do not accept enough? *(laughs)* I accepted it and then there is no problem. If you accept there will be no problem. If you accept "I am free," then you are free. If you accept "I am not free," you are not free.

• • •

Yesterday you said everyone must one day face the Truth. If I freely believe, then I am enlightened?

No! I AM does not need your belief or disbelief! From the I AM there is no difference. Fully accept I AM, that's all. If you have some grades of acceptance, that is, "Slowly I will try to accept, I will practice to accept," then you will slowly accept. It depends on you. It will not change.

Enlightenment will not change today, tomorrow, the next day. It is the same. Get it now, or after one year, or in this life span. It will not change.

You are not accepting it. Accept it fully and where is the problem? You are already free. Who tells you that you are not free? You are not opening to it. You are afraid to even utter "I am free." I do not know what that fear is.

When people say, "I am bound, I am suffering, I am miserable," then they feel free to speak. "I am free! I am deathless!" nobody speaks. Whose fault is this? Whatever you say, whatever you think, is going to happen. It will be fulfilled, now or tomorrow. If you think "I am free," then you are free.

People don't fully desire freedom. How many people desire freedom? I tell you that you are already free and you don't accept it. You want to do something. Freedom doesn't need any effort. Other things may need effort. Freedom is free. Free of your efforts.

So no more struggle, just accept it.

Then it will be there. When you don't make any effort it is there. When you try to catch it, it goes further away, because you are making an effort for the thing that is already there.

That is what I have learned from you. I am so thankful.

(laughs) Very nice. You learned it here, then your work is finished. If you don't make any effort whatsoever you are that itself.

• • •

This desire for freedom and the thought "Who am I?"—are they the same?

Same. Same. "Who am I?" brings you back if you have the desire for freedom. To whom did this desire arise? "To me" you say. Then find out who you are.

Freedom is faith in the present moment?

Why faith in present? In present moment, who is there to have faith in whom? In the present, to have faith is always something of the past. How can you have faith in the present moment? When the word *faith* comes, it takes you to the past.

I wanted to say that faith means to see that there is nothing else but the present moment.

Yes. That's right. The present moment is freedom. Look into the present moment. Freedom itself. You are always looking into the past moments. When did you give occasion to the present moment to manifest? You have never given a chance to this present moment. Always you are related to the past only. You are not giving your thought to this instant. This instant is the present moment. Look into it. Then you will see your face.

When you use this word *I,* then stop and look where this *I* arises from. This is the present moment. Look at this *I* and you will know this present moment, and then what is your faith? Where does it arise? If you go forward, you will go to the past. Return back to this, to where the thought *I* arose. Return back from whatever place to there.

• • •

You are free always! You don't have to run anywhere for freedom. You have to run for something else. Where is freedom, enlightenment, peace, bliss? It is here. Now, to be here, what effort is needed? You do not have to do anything to stay as you are.

Where can you turn? You only have to turn when you are somewhere else. To turn from where? When you are at home no flight is needed. Just remove these wrong ideas that you have borrowed from someone else, from society, your parents, your religion. It is not your nature to be unhappy or to suffer.

Does it go quickly or slowly, slowly?

Slowly is only the mind that fools you. To be right now, what understanding is needed? To be right now, what you already are, you don't need any understanding or misunderstanding.

Why did I come here then?

You came *here* because you thought you were *there!*

• • •

When I look in your eyes I see just Self. And I realize that when I honor you, I am honoring Self. But I still haven't learned to honor the Self in everyone. I can honor it in you but I still make comparisons and judgments of others. I don't see the Self in everyone.

First you have to see the Self within *you!* Then within me, and then everywhere else.

But when I look in other people's eyes I can't see it so clearly.

First see the Self within you. Then you will see that the Self in you is not other than the Self in me; it is the same Self. Then you perceive that the same Self in you, in me, is everywhere else. And Self alone is that Self. There is nothing apart from the Self. This experience you will surely get if you stick to Self alone. Nothing else ever existed at all!

But I—

OK, let's tackle it another way. When you see the Self, don't see the "not-Self" also at the same time. If you do not see the not-Self here and there and everywhere, what will you see?

Only the Self.

Only the Self everywhere! The not-Self doesn't exist. And the Self is not absent at all! So you will see Self everywhere. When I say everywhere, it is nowhere. Nowhere itself. Because no distance is involved. No here and somewhere. Self alone is total awareness of Self.

And all that waves and eddies and drops and bubbles, all are just the ocean. So, according to your question, "I see the ocean," is saying, "I see the ocean within myself but not in the waves or other eddies, tides, bubbles. There I do not see." So you have to see first the ocean within the ocean, Self within the Self. And this will include everything else. You will contain everything.

The Self contains everything. There is nothing apart from it. This is why you can call it emptiness. There is nothing beyond emptiness. All are empty. Nothing ever exists.

And when you see something existing, it is not other than you. So wherever there is an idea or concept of duality, of something else, there is confusion there about this. There is no duality at all. Oneness and wholeness is all.

If we accept duality, then there must be frontiers between the two, and then it cannot be limitless. There will be a division between duality and union. So there cannot be any divisions or frontiers in limitless reality or in Truth or emptiness. There are no frontiers. So this is seeing Self everywhere!

• • •

I have just come from a very busy culture and a very busy life in San Francisco—a life and culture filled with stress, noise, choices, confusion, and so much doing and activity. Suddenly, I come here and suddenly, there is just Self. Everything turns back to the Self. It is so simple. I am struck by the simplicity of your guidance. Just immediately! So simple. Just paying attention to the Self. How will it be when I go back to San Francisco?

Simplicity will not be lost. You cannot lose simplicity. Simplicity is nature.

We forget that.

It will not forget you. You may forget her, but she will not forget you. She is very chaste.

I will try to remember that.

It is the easiest and simplest of everything that you do, even easier than breathing. Easier than the breath that you inhale or exhale. For here you are neither to inhale nor exhale. Where does the inhalation and exhalation take place? You inhale, and it stops. You exhale, and it stops. And there, this is what you are. In between the inhaling and exhaling. Not even the effort to inhale or exhale is needed.

Or, from where does thought arise? There must be some activity for the thought to arise and go somewhere. But the source doesn't go, doesn't come—it is as it is. How simple it is. *(much laughter)* I have to laugh sometimes because I see fish in the river crying, "I am thirsty." "I want enlightenment," is the same thing. *(more laughter)*

What is near and easy you don't pay any attention to. What is difficult and far—the moon, Mt. Everest—you are attentive to. No one has arrived at the Self this way.

• • •

Who am I? Investigate it. Start with the question itself. First investigate *who.* Next, investigate *am.* Next, investigate *I.* When you return to the *I,* the question will disappear and no answer will be there.

That is your answer. That no answer is the answer. The river returns to the source from which it arises—the ocean—and disappears. No further inquiry to search for the river is needed. The river becomes the source.

We are all returning to the source. Every sentence that we speak returns. Every activity is moving towards itself. You only have to be aware and your journey will be ended. We are in the source itself. Even if you don't try, you are already there. Make this choice. Choose "I am free," and you are free. Choose "I am bound," and you are bound.

It is your choice. You choose to be bound. You choose to suffer. So if you have the choice, choose happiness and freedom. Let it be a good choice of love.

When all other choices have failed miserably and the result is suffering, we have been cheated. So let us go the other way. Nothing known has ever given us lasting happiness so far. Anything known is not permanent. Anything that has name and form is not permanent. Let us try nameless and formless emptiness this time, in this blessed span of life.

• • •

I make it so complicated when I think "What is the Self?" You make it sound so simple. You say "I AM the Self."

Yes. This simplicity is too difficult for you to digest.

I am looking for a concept of Self instead of I AM the Self.

You need not make any speculation or conceptualization. This is the doer itself and you have to agree. You cannot disagree. Can you speak to anyone else and say, "I am not Self?" And if you do, what will he think of you? *(laughs)*

When you are through the word *I* you are complete. *I* contains everything. It is sufficient. If you call yourself by the name *I* there will be no difficulty. You will be eternity. No death can touch you. Just remain *I.* That's all you have to do. How difficult is it? What is the difficulty in baptizing yourself "I am I"? That's all.

That simplifies it.

Too simple to accept?

Doubt, Fear, and Impediments

This morning I was lying on my bed and I had many doubts about what I am doing here and many, many thoughts. And suddenly I felt, "But what is this? I am lying on the bed and that is it." All the doubts suddenly went away and I felt very calm inside.

That is present moment. How long did you stay in present moment and what did you do to lose it?

I tried to analyze what had happened.

Whatever is too near is difficult to attend to. The eyes see everything. But the eyes do not see themselves. Like this, the Self through the mind sees all the world, but the mind doesn't return back home to be the Self.

How do we overcome fear?

By giving up all practices in that direction.

At that moment when the fear is thick—(snaps fingers)—*what do you do?*

At that moment between when you placed your fingers together and the snap, what did you do? Where did the sound of the snap come from?

This sound came from undoing it. Do it *(places fingers in position for snap)*, then undo. All that you have done, heard, seen, and read—for a moment, forget about this and tell me what is your face? What do you see? By simply undoing, what do you arrive at?

Nothing.

Ah. That is the return to your question: how to do? Undo and where do you arrive? A distance between thought and thought. This dive is the same as nothingness. When you are absolutely happy, this is the same as nothingness.

When you are absolutely happy to meet your beloved after twenty years, what is the thought in your mind? No thought.

Surrounded by nothingness you have to do nothing. You have to do nothing to be who you are. Nothing at all.

To become something, of course, to become a doctor is different. This is not a return to your true nature. You are always here. You deny it. You don't accept your greatness.

Being eternity itself, Reality itself, how can you say, "I am suffering in this body?"

What can you do without *I?* Wherever you go, who is there? You can't lose this even in suffering. "I suffer," you say. Try to leave. Breath in breath, who is more related to you?

• • •

I am feeling much fear and vulnerability. I understand that the world is a projection, yet I feel this fragmentation.

This fear is due to the first shock of wisdom, of light. It is as if this room is closed for the last twenty years, and you enter this dark room with a torch in hand to locate the light switch. This darkness has been established for twenty years. Instantly the light is there. The darkness is confused. Fear of disappearance is there.

After twenty years of darkness how much time should it take when you face the light? What has happened? Fear in the mind of darkness. In an instant it cannot be there when you face the light. The darkness of the room does not go in installments. You think you have been here for twenty years in darkness. That fear is ingrained in you. You have been living for millions of years like this, millions of years.

This fear of facing the light is not a fear like other fears. This is a fear of eternity. Eternal ocean of nectar, and you are swimming holding onto darkness.

Somehow you get a push, or you intend to jump into the ocean of immortality yourself. In between leaving this place of darkness and the leap, fear arises.

Without touching the light and after leaving the darkness, you can neither return back nor have you yet touched the surface. In this instant there is what can be called fear. Fear to leap into eternity because "I will lose this body consciousness, this darkness." This is only the fear of facing the light. You will become nectar itself, no death at all.

• • •

I have an impediment. This impediment is a doubt and it keeps me from loving you fully. It is giving me a headache.

What kind of headache do you have? There are two kinds

that I know of. One is from carrying a load on your head. The other is from having the load removed. If you suddenly have no load on your head, this can seem disorienting; you lose your balance and have a headache. No load can also seem like a headache.

There was once a wealthy man who knew he was to die. He had never prepared himself spiritually, never meditated. So he hired twenty workers from the marketplace to meditate for him. He said, "I will give you double wages and feed you your meals."

The workers were very excited. They wanted to begin right away but did not know what to do. "Just sit like this," the man told them as he showed them the meditation posture.

After a few hours, the workers rebelled. "Keep your double wages," they said. "This will make us sick, sitting here doing nothing." And so they quit.

So I don't know what kind of headache you have, but I suggest you give up the very idea of impediment. This idea in itself is now the only impediment. The scriptures say there are certain impediments to give up. First is the idea of a personal identity, a personality, name and form, as to who you are. Give this up, detach from it.

Next is the idea of heaven after you die. The idea of merit and demerit, that action will get you anywhere. Give up this attachment as well.

And then God. Give up your attachment to God itself. The idea that there is some agency outside of yourself that can help you now. Give this up.

And then give up the very idea of giving up! This must also be abandoned!

Yesterday, you said, "Tie up your camel and pray to Allah." I say now, ride your camel and forget about Allah! Ride the camel and you need not pray. If you tie it, you will have to untie it. If you tie it to a tree, you are also tied to it, so who will pray to Allah?

Impediment is only retaining the idea of impediment. The idea of the disappearance of impediment is the last impediment. This is the last hurdle, the last rung, the last leap forward.

Yes, there is a leap and there is the fear of emptiness—no name, no form. There is the fear of embracing this emptiness. You don't see anything there. Unknown! Absolutely empty! You need courage to hug that emptiness of no name and no form. Nobody can help you. Help can take you to the edge. But no one can help you here. The idea that there is help is itself an impediment. Throw away everything in name and form, *and jump!*

• • •

I always seem to give rise to more questions and doubts.

One day the king said to his minister, "Go out at dawn and find the first person that you meet, and I will give him a kingdom."

The minister went out at dawn and the first person he met was a beggar. He took this beggar to the palace and sat him on the throne. He was bathed and clothed and fed a royal feast. But soon the beggar asked, "Where is my begging bowl? It is time for me to beg."

While sitting on the throne he still had the idea of a begging bowl. Who can help that beggar-king put down his begging bowl? Such is the case with you.

I get to the edge and my head tells the feet to jump but my feet don't go. The courage doesn't get to the feet. Is there anything I could do, or not do, that might get the courage to the feet?

Neither! Neither doing or not doing. Do not allow your mind to abide anywhere, not even in the nothingness.

• • •

What is it that takes birth then?

Unfulfilled samskaras take birth.

And the Self?

The Self is not touched. Only the body is born and dies. Your cumulative samskaras give rise to the impetus for another lifetime. This unceasing rebirth is called samsara. It is suffering. This goes on until enlightenment.

Enlightenment is the fire of knowledge which burns the samskaras and then your birth and death problems end.

You say the body is like a dress?

Anything that you call "my"—such as "my body, my house, my car, my sweater, my wife." What is the difference? To whom does this body belong? Who is it that wears the body? My mind, my intellect, my memories, my dress—whose are they? Who are you, to whom these things belong?

The body is different. The body is a part of you, whereas the car, the dress, the sweater are not.

Anything that is real must stay the same always. Now, for the dress—when you sleep, where is the dress and where is the body? When you sleep, who is present? The body is not there, nor the dress, nor the sweater. Who is it to whom all these belong? Ask yourself, "Who am I?" Then you will know what the body is, what the mind is, and what all these possessions are.

Well, I could just let it go—

No, no! I am not asking you to let go. I am asking you to see. If I say "your sweater," or "your pants," where does your mind cling? Where do you run to cling?

To the sweater.

OK. Now ask, "Who am I?" Go and cling to *I* and then report what you are clinging to. "Who am I?" In this, *I* is an object. Let this object be clung to. Let your mind go towards the Self and cling and tell me what it is.

You are returning the thought to the place from where it arises. "My thought, my mind"—return these things to the place from where they spring forth. Return to the origin of the thought itself, and you will find *I*. Then we can speak of the body and mind, but first you must know who you are. Everything else will be easy after that.

First locate where you are and then we can find the distance to where we have to proceed. Let us see where we are just now, on the map, and then we will see where we have to go. *I* is a place where you presently are, isn't it?

Yes.

So find out, let your thought go towards the *I* and see what happens.

Empty!

Ah. Right, right, very good answer. So *I* is empty. You send your mind to find the source of the *I,* the source of your being, the source of everything, and you said "empty."

Now, from this emptiness let us proceed. First you turned to face the light. You turned to face yourself. From there, from emptiness, now face the other side, the wrong side, where you see bodies, sweater, house, car, wife. You slowly step out of this emptiness and tell me what you see. You see it from emptiness now. What are you going to see?

Now.

Emptiness is always now, yes. Never then. So step out of this now. Proceed out of now and tell me where you go. Beyond this instant, what do you see?

(long silence) *I feel thoughts coming up.*

Let them come. Within emptiness, thoughts come. Within emptiness, what do they represent? Within the ocean, waves come. What do they represent? Within the emptiness, thoughts come. What do they represent?

The mind?

From the ocean waves arise, stay, move, and fall.

Still emptiness.

Good. All the waves that come from emptiness must be empty. Just as the waves that come from the ocean must be water only. They cannot be stones. Now, you bring a thought from emptiness which is not empty. Try it and investigate.

There is nothing there!

Very good. You have done the job. And that is your nature. This is what you are. You have to wake up. You are consciousness. You are empty. You are just in this moment only. Whenever you see name and form you are sleeping. What do you see in the world without name and form?

Where is consciousness as pure, immaculate eternity, permanent happiness, love and bliss? When you look from there, from emptiness, you see everything. Nothing beyond that. Nothing to do. Only to be as you are.

We have misconceived ourselves, that we have been born and we are the body and we are suffering and we have to die. Where it comes from nobody knows; it is just a concept. It is not real. You have been trained by your family, your society, your religion. Yet this emptiness is your own nature. This is what you are, and really you need not do anything about it. You need not do penance or retire to a cave.

This is what you have to understand. I now answered your question from your own mind. If you see from emptiness, you will just see the waves of the ocean. And this is your projection. When you wake up and say "I am Ken," instantly there is samsara. Only your projection. When you don't give rise to a thought, you return to emptiness, to consciousness. When one thought arises, the world rises. One thought is the world.

And even this is just your projection and not other than you, as you are one. Just as your eyes, your ears, your hands are not apart from you.

This is how the world is. All the beings, the birds, the flowers, the rocks—all you, your Self. If somehow you understand it, where is the suffering? Suffering is always something else. Then only you suffer. When your total being is there and this total being is empty, then there will be no trouble.

So understand this, that this is who you are already. This is your own nature. You are that. You are already your own nature. You are that. You do not have to attain or acquire it.

We get preoccupied.

Yes. This preoccupation is death. If you know that all of this is me, then there will be no preoccupation and no past either. Do not fragment yourself into parts. Expand your understanding beyond limits. "I am so and so" is enough limitation to suffer.

Bondage arises only when you fragment yourself. You become the part and leave the rest and then try to understand. This is a drop of the ocean thinking, "I am separate from the ocean. I suffer and I must go on moving on the surface of the ocean. Always I am in fear of breakage, fear of a larger wave, so many fears."

There is no peace or safety in being free from the ocean or in running from the ocean. Not knowing that I am the same as the ocean creates confusion, suffering, and fear.

So long as we think, we will suffer. This samsara comes from one thought: "I am Ken." There is no difference between Ken and the whole of samsara. Can you separate Ken from samsara? When Ken proceeds to the source, then everything will be solved.

I find myself running away from myself. It becomes compli-cated. I forget.

Yes, yes. You forget. You only need yourself. Forget that you need a mirror. All that you see is only a reflection. When you remove this mirror, where does Ken disappear to?

Still here.

Yes. That mirror where you saw your face, remove it. That face is here. Reject this mirror. See who you are. Return to the place from where this thought arises.

Myself, emptiness, consciousness—same thing. You can't step out of it. It's always there. We only think it is not there, therefore we search. Sometimes I am searching for glasses with which to read. Searching for the glasses while wearing them. I search everywhere and don't find them. I see everything and don't find them. Through the glasses I am looking, because without the glasses I can't see, I can't search. Yet I can't see the glasses, I can't find them out there.

You are searching—"I want to be free." Through this thought you are searching for freedom. You will get it. This thought itself is the same as what you are searching for. This is consciousness! *(laughs)*

Where does consciousness go when I sleep?

How do you know it goes anywhere? When you wake up and you speak and then you sleep again, was this conscious-ness of sleep there or not? You say, "I had a very good sleep, no disturbance." Is it not consciousness when the body sleeps? Who is enjoying it? Consciousness of waking and consciousness of sleeping—no difference.

States pass in front of you as projected pictures pass along the screen. The screen is inactive and does not change. Whenever there is movement, there must be something that does not move. Identify yourself with the screen itself.

You are the screen, or the substratum, on which these states appear. And that is unseen. When you see something, the screen is not seen; when you see the screen, nothing is seen. When the screen is seen, the pictures are not seen.

When you are conscious you don't see the projections of name and form. Wherever you see name and form you don't see Reality.

For example, there are several images made of gold. One image is of Christ, one is of a dog, and one is of a pig. Each is 200 grams of gold. If you take one to a jeweler to melt it, which will fetch the best price? Pig, dog, or a god, same price. If you value the essence, same value. Essence is the same. If you remove name and form, nameless and formless, what are you? Who are you?

Are you saying gold is like the Self?

Yes, but because we are involved with name and form we see the pig or the god. The moment we go back to the source and recognize the essence, the gold, the Reality, the emptiness—this is nirvana! If we stay with the recognition of only the name and form—samsara! Reject the name and form and immediately—nirvana.

• • •

What is karma?

I don't believe in karma. There is no past karma, no present karma, and no future karma. A man has three wives. One he is married to for ten years, one he is married to in the present, and another he will marry very soon.

Just before the last marriage he dies. With his death all three wives are widowed. With enlightenment, the same thing happens to the past, present, and future karmas.

If the doer is not there, the karmas are like widowed wives. His ego is dead now. This man who has no doubt has no karma. He has found liberation here and now. He is not born, not incarnated. It is what has been all the time; no changes have occurred.

The wives are widowed, and the liberated man is free and can do what he likes. It leaves no impression and so forms no karma.

Often in the spiritual scene this idea has led to permissiveness, license, harmfulness, and misunderstanding.

I am speaking of the non-doer. For the doer there will be a reaction and he will have to pay for it. One who is involved in attachments will reap the consequences of his thoughts and concepts. You become what you think.

In the dream somebody becomes a beggar and somebody else a king. But both belong to a dream. Nobody is a beggar or king. Once you recognize that you are neither, you are free.

We have a conception that by practice we shall become free. Such a person is postponing his freedom. We become enlightened in this instant only and not as a result of ten years' practice. Freedom is available now.

• • •

*When I ask myself what this whole spiritual journey is about,
I say it is nothing more than getting rid of all concepts. Am I right?*

Spirituality doesn't tell you to get rid of anything. What
will be removed? Where will you put it? In this world there are
mountains and rivers and animals. If you get rid of them,
where will they go? They have to stay here. It is better to stay
with everything and with love, not to reject or accept.

Be your own Self. These things are not apart from your
own Self. They are within you. Change only your viewpoint.
Accept these things within your own Self as your own Self.
Why not accept that all of this is me? This is a fact.

Even the hopes and concepts?

Yes. If you accept these as within you, where is the trouble?
There is trouble only when we accept differences between ourselves and something or someone else. Accept that everything
is within you as your own Self. Emptiness. Eternity. Whatever
you call it. Everything is within that, and you are one with
that. Then what will you reject? Where will you send these
things?

You are whole. Where will you send anything? "I AM
ALL!" is the teaching of the Upanishads. All this is myself.
Spirituality doesn't tell you to let go.

But let's try a different way. If you let go of everything,
then what is left? What will be left?

You can't reject anything from the Self. If you reject, there
will be frontiers between you and the Self. If you say "Let go,"
there will be frontiers between you and the things you have
thrown out. So it is not possible in the Truth to have any
limitation, any frontier. It is whole! Either you reject every-

thing, or you accept everything as yourself. Whatever suits you, you can do. Then you keep quiet. Become empty of thoughts and accept everything.

• • •

How can I remove the fear?

What fear can you have? It may be fear of the destruction of everything that you are holding. Fear that you will lose all the holdings of your mind. So you are caught in between. On the one side, you can see the destruction of everything your mind has clung to, all of your holdings. On the other side, eternity is calling you. You don't like to go back, and yet you hesitate to embrace eternity. This is a transit period only. A transit camp. A flight will be announced. You can't go back. The plane you arrived on is gone and you are in the transit lounge. Wait for the call, that's all.

Since you know it is a transit lounge in which you are sitting, do not become attached to anything. This is only a transit lounge. No one will be here, and no one has been here. Do not become attached here. Let go of everything so that you can travel comfortably.

All samsara is a transit lounge; nothing is permanent. Everyone is shifting. Some are coming, some are waiting for the call. You are very fortunate to know that you are in the transit lounge. Get ready. Don't be attached to anything. You have to return home.

• • •

The mind and body seem to be a distraction from Reality, and need a special atmosphere.

He who cannot digest anywhere needs a special atmosphere. Mind needs some abode. Otherwise there is no mind. The thought "I want to be free" brought you here. And still you are holding onto that thought. *(laughs)*

Something beyond that also is what brought me here.

This desire must dissolve now. You are abiding in that desire now, and that won't do.

If you are on the plains and there is scorching heat, you desire to go up into the mountains. Then the desire to avoid the heat leads you to want to go to the snows. You want to go to the higher altitude to be comfortable. In every step the heat is left behind. You go on climbing, climbing. The heat is leaving you by itself. In this desire to go to the better climate, the idea "I am hot" is completely released.

Now, here you are holding onto the concept of freedom.

But this holding on also helps me to focus on the distant mountains.

It has already helped. It has brought you here already. That idea has to disappear itself. If it is not going, you are clinging. Then, clinging to this clinging, you forget what you came here for.

You can only hold one thing at a time. When the concept of bondage brings you to freedom, then give up this concept.

Very often I feel unfree and then I feel unhappy.

That's right. Just remove *un* from your language. Why do you use *un* unnecessarily? If you don't use *un*, then you speak the correct language.

Then there is no trouble.

Ah. So who imposed trouble on whom?

I imposed trouble on myself.

No, no. This *un* imposed trouble. So why do you use *un* then?

Because that's the way I feel.

OK. Give up this feeling.

How do I do that?

By not doing it.

To me that is very hard work.

What is?

To not do that.

No, no. You asked how to do it. I said by not doing it you have done it. Then don't do. If you don't do, what's there?

The feeling will disappear.

And what is left?

Nothing.

Ah. In nothingness, are you happy or unhappy?

I think I am happy.

Think?

I hope!

When you say "nothing," then no thinking and no hope is there. In happiness there is no thinking at all. In unhappiness there is thinking. In any kind of happiness there is no thinking at all.

When you are happy, do you think?

No.

When you don't think, you are happy. When you are happy, you don't think.

Yes.

So what effort do you need to make to be happy? What effort do you suggest?

This is difficult for me to understand.

Understanding is not necessary to be happy. One wants a moment of peace; then one wants to stay there and extend the moment into duration.

Don't try to understand. You are in trouble because you

want to understand. Give up understanding this freedom. When you want to understand, this is bondage. Objects can be understood. When there is neither subject nor object, how can you understand?

Not possible.

No need to understand.

Master, why are there so many books and scriptures on understanding? Even books on Ramana, just to understand.

These are nets to catch the fish who are now going to search for enlightenment. Few fish are going for enlightenment, so there is a very big net to catch these few fish in the vast waters of the ocean of bondage. Scriptures are another net to catch the fish who have avoided other nets. Now they are caught in the scripture net, which has a very fine mesh.

Another net of bondage?

The last net is scriptures; God is the last hurdle. When you renounce everything, then you are free. Free of God, free of scriptures, free of samsara.

What you have studied must be forgotten. Then you can leap forward. You cannot leap forward if you cling to the understanding of the scriptures. Then you discover that you are not to try to understand. This is leaping forward beyond scriptures. No difference in holding scriptural concepts than in holding worldly knowledge.

What happens if you are in samadhi state and you think it is freedom?

When do you think this? Before samadhi, after samadhi? Not in samadhi. So this samadhi must be constant so you do not think anything else but freedom.

So first, where do these concepts of freedom and bondage come from? Not to gain freedom, but to undo what you have already done.

But undoing or giving up is also doing.

Emptiness is the natural position. If I try to hold, I have added something into emptiness. Now I undo what I have done before. *(takes a wad of paper that he is holding and opens his hand, letting it fall to the floor)* What I held I have given up. The concept of bondage is not your nature. Your nature is always freedom.

With my intellect, I see that very clearly, but still—

No, no. Your nature itself is freedom. You would not seek freedom if it were not your nature. You would not search.

Everybody wants to return home. Everybody wants to return to their true nature. Freedom is your nature. Anything that you have imposed on yourself to be unhappy, to be bound, is a concept. It is an imaginary concept, so give it away. Then you can't say "I am doing something."

Suppose you have such a strong imagination that you believe you see a ghost in a room. Then someone comes to ward off the ghost. This person says the ghost is removed. There was neither a ghost nor a removal. This is the return to your natural state.

So from the beginning this has been your problem. Now how should we solve this important problem? Undoing is also a doing. Better not to try. Just not to understand this thing. Undo now means you forget everything that you have read, heard, seen, felt. That is returning to freedom. Everything else has been imposed on you. All knowledge is imposed by society, parents, church.

I feel like I can't even return to freedom because it is already there.

OK, yes. Then stop here and don't keep trying to understand it. That's all. If you try to understand it, then it starts again.

I feel that someone has hit me on the head.

This is a gentleman's hit. Don't try to understand it.

We feel it takes effort to not think and that it is natural to have desires. But it is really just the reverse, just the opposite of that. That is the illusion! That keeps us bound.

• • •

Questions arise and then I follow the thought to its source. From emptiness there are no questions.

When you arrive at the Self, when was it that you were not the Self? You don't need to understand anything. When you try to understand there arises the function of the mind. This function of the mind is the doing that takes you in the wrong direction.

Mind and Killing the Ego

Papaji, a recurring difficulty for me is that my ego wants to be part of the process of becoming free. My ego want to congratulate itself by saying, "Look at me. Look at what I am doing."

Part of me says, "No, you're not coming here," but my ego, feeling like a little child, says, "Me, too! I'm coming too!" So there isn't quite that letting go.

No need for letting go. You should make use of this very sympathetic ego. It is a nice ego, a good ego. If the ego wants to be free, it is a good symptom. First, the ego will start.

Usually, the ego doesn't want you to be free, and will tend to take you toward the objects of the senses. Mostly for enjoyment.

If the ego wants to be free, start with the ego itself. First, *I* is an ego, isn't it?

Yes.

Through this ego you are working. Everything is being worked by the ego itself in the world. Now you have to make use of this ego. Take this ego Selfward from where it arises. If she wants to be free, take this ego toward freedom. What is that? Return to its source.

Ego is a thought, isn't it? Ego is the first thought that rises in the morning. "I am Fred" is Fred-thought. So dive this ego-thought toward where it rises.

I has taken a role of ego itself. *I*, the real *I*, has become *I* as an ego. "I am doing this; I have done that; I want that; I don't want this; I know." These thoughts rise as the ego.

Then, turn the ego back towards its source from where it rises. "My ego wants to be free," you said. So bring this ego back to its source. Then this ego-I will introduce you to the real source, also an *I*. When she returns to her source, this *I* will merge into the source. That is why this thought is a very blessed thought.

"I want to be free" is still ego appearing. So you must work on this ego-thought, this *I*-thought. And return back to its source. Then the ego will see her face; she will merge and ego will vanish. What will be left is the source itself. And this ego will not appear again. It will be dissolved . . . discharged into the ocean as a river discharges into the ocean and becomes ocean and does not return.

From there, the functions will be from the source itself! Not egoistic. Spontaneous, without involvement in the thought process. No thought process will be there—only direct spontaneous activity without thinking.

First *I* think and then *I* act. This process will be gone and direct activity will be there according to circumstances. In this process even the memory won't be there either. You don't need memory. Memory is ego itself.

All this will be finished. Mind will be no-mind. Mind and ego, there is not much difference. Neither the mind nor the ego exist. In fact, they never existed!

These are just your own desires. Desires for the enjoyment of the samsara. Yet in reality, they don't exist. You have never seen the face of your ego, nor the face of your mind. It is like a ghost, so as a ghost we accept it. This has been handed down from generation to generation. In reality, the ego doesn't exist, the mind doesn't exist, and samsara doesn't exist.

Yet when the ego rises, samsara rises. When the ego ceases, samsara ceases. When samsara ceases, then you will recognize your nature. You are not to earn it by any effort!

Even when you meditate it is the suggestion through the ego itself that you meditate.

The way you speak about it now, it sounds like a very loving process. Normally, I think of getting rid of the ego or killing the ego, to let it go. But now you are saying that one should let the ego see its own true nature.

Yes.

That seems like an incredibly loving thing to do for anything. Because then it isn't killing but an enhancement. Whatever sees its own true nature would be perfect.

When you decide to kill ego, this is the ego itself. How will you kill it? Has anybody killed the ego? What is the weapon needed to kill the ego? First there must be something to be killed. First you must see the thing that is to be killed. Then, in the seeing, it is already killed.

This thought arises: "I want to kill the ego." Trace this *I* itself. When you say, "I want to kill the ego," return back to this *I* and see if there is any ego to be killed.

You have often said the ego is like a wave arising in the ocean. It seems to me that the ocean and the ego are part of the same thing. Now I see I should really sink into my ego and from the place of the ego recognize that I am of the ocean itself.

No, not that way. When you say the wave belongs to the ocean, who is saying the wave is different from the ocean?

Ego.

Ego is the wave. You are the source. You are ocean, yet you do not identify yourself with the ocean in that place. When you are the ocean, how do you differ from the waves? What conflict do you have with the waves?

None. But my problem is to go from the ego to the source.

This source is ocean itself. Ego plays on the surface of the ocean like a wave. The trouble is that right now you are describing yourself as an onlooker of both ocean and wave, standing somewhere on the beach. You have to identify yourself and say, "I am the ocean."

I see. I thought I was seeing myself as the wave. But if I really saw myself as the wave then I wouldn't be separate from the ocean. So the wave can't see itself as separate from the ocean.

You have to be ocean itself. You are the ocean. When a wave arises, you be under the wave. How is the wave different from the ocean itself? Name, shape, and movement. All this is activity, but how is the ocean concerned with the wave's name, form, or movement?

Waves rise and fall and move about, and how is this the ocean's concern? You be the ocean first and then see. Where is the wave? Where is your ego?

These waves are only samsara rising from the ocean. Underneath is nirvana. Ocean is nirvana. Emptiness. In that emptiness waves arise. And in emptiness if waves are moving, how are they different from emptiness itself? They are *all* empty!

So you have to return to the source, to emptiness, to the ocean, and then see how you feel, how you are different in activities, movement, name, form.

• • •

What is your response to someone who says, "I have a family and children. I have too many commitments, so what possibility is there for me to awaken?"

That person must wake up from the dream that he or she has a family. One is always free and one is always alone. The mind is only dreaming. For example, when I fall asleep I dream that I marry and have children. In the dream I start to worry that I have no time for meditation or to go to the cave in the mountains. All these things are uttered when a person is living in a dream. It is better to wake that person up from the dream. Nothing has ever touched this person; he or she is always alone. When you see any name or any form, it is only a dream.

• • •

I read that the Maharshi said we should constantly abide in the Self.

I would say instead, liberate the mind from any abiding.

But the mind does not abide.

Who else but the mind abides?

Yes, but the mind finishes.

Yes, this is non-abidance. If you abide somewhere, you have rejected someplace else to abide here. If you abide here, the mind will jump to abide somewhere else as well. Allow the mind to abide nowhere and what will be the result? Mind has to abide on an object. If the object is removed, the mind cannot hang with an object. Then there will be no-mind.

Then the mind is its object.

Yes, same thing. Any object is objectified mind. And if you don't allow the mind to abide anywhere, there is no-mind. No-mind is freedom. When mind abides, samsara appears. Samsara is a construction of the mind.

Thinking and Emptiness

A woman is about to be married. As was normal for someone in this condition, her head was filled with thoughts and plans and ideas for the future. She was walking from her village through the forest to the next village when a lion jumped into the middle of the road.

In that moment where is her mind? Where is her past? Where are her thoughts and plans for the future?

The future is dependent on the past. The mind is a graveyard digger! Digging up old bones from the past to chew on! So welcome the lion in your path.

I think I experience emptiness, but it's heavy.

Emptiness is not heavy. This cannot be true emptiness. Who is thinking? Where does this *I* live that thinks? For you *I* is also a thought. Trace it back to its source and discover from where it arises. The thought must stop. First, no object, no doing, no *I*.

This is why I do not give you a practice. If you practice meditation for one hour or two hours, for a ten-day retreat or a one-month retreat, then what about the rest of the year? It *must* be sixty seconds each minute, sixty minutes of each hour, twenty-four hours a day.

That is true silence. That is true meditation. True meditation never stops! This is why there is nothing to do. No practice. Simply be who you already are!

I am giving you nothing and taking away nothing, only pointing to that which you already are. Don't leave here thinking, "I think I experienced emptiness."

First remove the activity or doing, which is thinking and experiencing, then remove the *I*. Then we can begin! Then there is room for interesting discussion. From this place report your reality.

• • •

I find that during satsang I fall asleep. It is pleasant but blank. Then I drift back into awareness. Should I make any effort to stay awake?

No. It is good to sleep during satsang. *(everyone laughs for several minutes)*

If you are awake in satsang and you fall asleep and again you are awake in satsang, how can the interval be called sleep? If you have a thought, "I am meditating," then a thought, "I am asleep," and then a thought, "I am meditating," how can you call it sleep? When you leave for sleep, where did you put the baggage of satsang?

It was still there.

Still there. And when you wake up, where did you leave this baggage of satsang—in sleep?

Still there.

Yes. This is consciousness. Consciousness does not sleep. In the waking state it is awake. In the sleeping state it is awake. This awareness does not change. The states may change. And you are that awareness, in waking state or sleeping state or dreaming state. There is no difference. Difference is created by the mind. And when in satsang, we do not speak our mind, only awareness. *(laughs)*

• • •

I have a question relating to freedom, about the use of the correct method in regard to the chakras.

Don't worry about methods. If you are sincere and honest, and have a true desire for freedom, even wrong methods will take you there. Therefore give rise to the desire 100% and the rest will take care of itself. What you are doing is not important; the end is important. You can do anything you like. The end must be that "I have to be free." You must be sincere, serious, and honest. Then don't worry about the methods. This inside Self is consciousness itself. If you do not know the correct method, it will lead *you*. Where you are arriving, it already knows who is coming, and it will go out to receive you in the proper way for you. You must be honest and never mind proper method.

I see that my mind is looking to own and control what is going on.

When the idea of control comes, the mind resists. Don't control the mind. Let it go anywhere it likes. Let it run anywhere in this moment and what happens?

It relaxes.

Why?

No tension. No fighting.

So this is the opposite method, letting the mind go where it likes. All of meditation is to control the mind, and this is letting the mind go. What difference does it make?

The result is the same.

Yes. Neither will work for some, both will work for some, one or the other will work for others. It is your earnestness, your desire, not the method.

You are always in the source. How can you leave the source? This is a joke. The fish are crying, "I am thirsty." You are crying like a fish. "I am not the source. I am not myself. I am not I AM." What a big joke. When you come here for freedom, it is a big joke. I myself enjoy this joke. You will return to where you came from.

Well, is there anything important then, Papaji?

This is the only thing that is important. Nothing else. Only this.

Well, if it is a joke, my coming here, what is the difference between an ordinary man and an enlightened man? Is there no difference?

One difference. What is this difference?

I don't know. I am not an enlightened man.

This is the same I AM who says, "I am not enlightened," or "I am enlightened." This I AM is the same.

But the experience of the enlightened man?

In I AM there is no experience. You only have to give up the experiences that I AM is not. "I am so and so." This is the experience. I AM, to have an experience, has become somebody. I AM is existence. I AM is awareness. Finish at the I AM and tell me what experience you will get.

And this I AM contains all the cosmos. So there is nothing to attain or do. Just end at I AM and see what the experience is. I AM is eternal. Here, death can't enter. It is here in waking, deep sleep, and dreaming. Nothing to lose or gain.

To become something, to expect something, you have to do something. To remain I AM you don't have to do anything. Its fullness is emptiness. I AM is the ocean, and the waves are the cosmos, the universe, all happenings. And you can enjoy. This is called Leela's sport.

• • •

When you give rise to a thought and don't cling to it, what happens? It returns to emptiness and so is no-thought. Only clinging creates unfulfilled desires.

If the thought arises, "I want to be free," it is not clinging, because freedom is not an object. Where does it spring from? It will merge there and you are conscious of that. Therefore it is called freedom. Effortless. No practice. Only see what is happening. Enough that you have attention and you are aware all the time. Even when you say "I was not aware," you were aware that you were not aware.

The mind has a tendency to make freedom an object.

If the king is gardening, he is not called a gardener. He is still a king.

Is awareness of no-thought still a subtle thought that has to be rejected?

Also rejected.

How do we do that?

By not raising this question. If you do not give rise to this question of how to do it, what is left?

Awareness.

And how did you "do it?" *(laughs)*

• • •

This is just a trick of the mind.

If you call it a trick it is no more a trick, is it? A trick is that which doesn't allow you to proceed further. This is called *Maya.* But it is imagination only. This is no trick. You want to stop. You do not want to proceed further, so you shift the responsibility to the trick. But this is no trick. *Being* is no trick. You are by nature as you are—this is no trick. What is called a trick is that you do not want to proceed further.

• • •

I used to have an image of flying though space and I was scared. Now that I know there is no place to land, I still have the image, but I am not scared anymore.

So, if you have nothing to fear, why don't you identify yourself as the space itself? You are already that. It is like the wave rejecting the ocean and trying to run away from it, isn't it? "I will save myself and go somewhere else." With great speed the wave rushes away from the ocean, from this great fear of the ocean. Always she abandons the ocean, what she has to do, what she has been doing, what she was. "I will save myself."

What is all this running to the shore? It has to merge into its own substratum, into its own essence. Only the separate name and form have to go to be recognized as the ocean itself.

So when the idea of space arises, identify yourself as that ocean, as space itself. Then you can shout, "I've got it!"

• • •

I find questions come up to ask you, but when I follow them back to their source they disappear.

When you know this trick you don't need to ask anything of anyone. When you know this simple trick you don't need to ask anything, anywhere. So stay there. That is your permanent, eternal abode. Where nothing can touch you.

When you don't stay home, you wander to the supermarket. And you make purchases and you like certain things and so you want to stay there. You want to stay on there. That is what is happening. All these problems you are facing are only at the supermarket. At home there is no problem. No trouble. If you go home too late, you will be pushed out and the gate will be closed. It will be too late for you to return home. So do it now. Finish making your purchases and return home now.

And this home which I mention is your own Self. It is eternity. Where there are no demands and no needs and no wants, and therefore no desires. Desire is only in the mind if something is absent. You desire that thing and you run out of the house after it. Your true home is perfect, complete by itself. No need is there, you see. It is complete fullness. Full of everything. You are the Lord of the place. Don't become a beggar. "I need this, I need that," is just begging about "things."

• • •

You said, "I am not an enlightened man." Where did you get this thought? Did you not go to the past? Who is not enlightened? Past or present?

Past.

Therefore you made an effort to go to the past—to get this concept of unenlightenment, ignorance. So don't make any effort to go to the past and let us see what happens. Don't make any effort to go to the past or to conceive of a future.

Who are you when there is no past or future? In that split moment you are enlightened. Now where will you go if you split this instant?

Try to become ignorant! Out of this instant of light, go into darkness.

I can't.

Not possible? Good. Stay as you are. No effort is needed. You have to go somewhere to become something else. When you know it is stupid to become something, this is enlightenment. For this you do not need any effort at all.

• • •

Why do you use the word emptiness *so much? You seem to really like the word* emptiness.

Everybody has some fascination about certain words. When I use this word, I speak from my experience, not for any other reason. This is my experience. And to represent that experience I don't find any appropriate word. It is an indescribable experience, where there is no trace of anything. Nothing. When I use the word *emptiness* it is the best word I can use for my experience. Nothing ever existed. You can call it empty. There is no other word available to my knowledge.

In 1919, after the first world war, I was a small boy going to school. We had a one-month vacation for the British victory. We were all given little badges and we were very happy.

My mother went to visit her sister in Lahore. I accompanied her. We were living a hundred miles towards the frontier. One evening we all went out together and we had mango shakes. Mango shakes were a common drink in the Punjab. We were sitting around a table and they were passing the mango shakes around the table. When my turn came I was in a situation I could not describe at that time. I had never heard of samadhi. But when they passed my glass I did not reach up to take it or say anything.

My mother grew very afraid for me. They carried me to a nearby mosque. Even though we were Hindus, we lived within a Muslim majority, and if you were sick you went to the mosque for help. Animal or man could be brought to the priest of the mosque and he would say some mantras.

So they carried me to the mosque where it was pronounced that I must be haunted by a ghost. This was reasonable to them because beyond this they did not know.

They brought me home and for the whole night I sat in stillness. The next morning I could again speak.

My mother asked me, "Why were you silent?" I said I did not know. Then she asked if I saw Krishna. I said, "No, nobody was there."

She wanted to know why I had been sometimes laughing and sometimes crying. What did I see? I told her I didn't see anything. That was the first time I experienced what we are speaking about. During that time I did not see anything; I was very happy. But to express that happiness, as I have been doing now for seventy years, whenever I sit, I go back to that space that is beyond time. To express that moment I use the word *emptiness,* but there was neither nothingness nor something-ness. Inside I was very conscious but I could not describe that consciousness by any name. Therefore I use the name *emptiness.*

So you could say "empty of name and form"?

Even empty of emptiness itself, let alone name and form. This word I borrowed from somewhere. I can't describe, I have no language to describe, but to speak to you I must use some word that you understand and that is *emptiness.*

There is no time concept. No light. No darkness. Only consciousness is there. And this consciousness cannot be grasped by any imagination. Vast emptiness.

What we speak about anybody can reasonably understand. And if it is understood it becomes a trap. Understanding and not understanding are all in the scheme of ignorance, just a realm of the mind. This is not learning. This is your birthright. You cannot study to be what you are. You do not need to understand in order to breathe.

• • •

Your talks remind me of the saying, "When a pickpocket meets the Buddha he only sees his pockets."

Well, I will tell you of a master pickpocket. This master pickpocket was in Lahore, which was a major diamond center. One day he saw a man buy the perfect diamond. This diamond was the one he had been waiting for all these years. This was the one diamond he had to have.

So the pickpocket followed the man who had bought the diamond. When the man bought a ticket on the train to Madras, the pickpocket also purchased a ticket to Madras, and ended up in the same compartment. When the man went to the toilet, the pickpocket searched everywhere. When the man went to sleep, the pickpocket continued to search for the diamond without luck.

Finally the train reached Madras, and the diamond merchant was on the platform. At this moment the pickpocket approached him.

"Excuse me, sir," he said. "I am a master pickpocket. I have tried everything without success. You have arrived now at your destination. I will not bother you. But I must know where you hid the diamond."

The man said, "I saw you watch me buy the diamond. When you showed up on the train, I knew you were after the diamond. I thought you must be very clever, and I wondered where I could hide this diamond that you would never search. So I hid it in your own pocket."

This diamond that you are searching for is so close, closer than the breath. But you search the Buddha's pockets. Empty everything from the pockets of your mind. Search where there is no distance and nothing to do. It is too easy for you.

• • •

You can only lose something that is in your pocket. You can only lose what you have gained. When you have an empty pocket, what can you lose? Then you need not have any fear. You can't lose emptiness. Nobody can pick the empty pocket! So empty your pocket. This is called *freedom*. Whatever is stored in the pocket, empty it. Then there is no fear. You can walk freely.

The Sanskrit word for meditation, *dyana*, means to empty the mind. When the mind is empty, when there is no concept in the mind, this is dyana. When dyana travels to China, with Bodidharma, the Chinese pronounce it *chan*, empty mind. The Japanese take the word *chan* and pronounce it *zen*. All empty mind with no thought whatsoever. When we meditate we watch the function of the mind so that it doesn't cling to any object.

When the policeman chases the thief, the thief runs away.

The policeman then tracks the thief back to his den, back to where he started from. Like this, as a thought arises chase it back to its den. This den is the source. It is the source of all the thieves who have been robbing you all these years. If you enter there, they will vacate the place.

When there are no thoughts left, the den is empty, and this emptiness is your nature. You will be very happy to settle down there. When you walk and talk now, you will function from this emptiness.

If you lose this, the ego arises from somewhere, and then you become egocentric and don't recognize who you are. Just this thought, "I am some name," is quite enough to fall back again into this.

Practice and Meditation

I don't find that *meditation* is really a suitable translation of *dyana*. In Pali, the Buddha's language, it was exported to China as *dana*, where it was pronounced *chan*, and in Japan it was called *zen*. People who practice, during meditation, as observer and as object of observation, actually come under *concentration,* or *darna* in Sanskrit. It is actually darna where the question of the observer and the object of observation arises.

Darna is good to bring the mind back to one object from its tendency to run about, object to object, many times in a second. So it can be good to bring it, by concentration, back to one object. This is just like holding the tail of a dog. As long as you hold it, it is straight. When you leave it, it becomes curly again. *(everyone laughs)* It is not the nature of the tail to be straight.

Dyana means there is no object or subject in the mind. All the rest is concentration of some sort. Concentration has to be practiced. In the practice the mind will never be destroyed. It may be calm for some time, as long as you are practicing, but it will not destroy itself. It will not be destroyed

So the question is whether to keep the mind calm by practice, or destroy it forever. The latter is absolutely necessary for freedom. When there is no mind, there is freedom! Concentration is practiced the world over, but I don't find any results from it. Concentrating on an object, like the breath or body, is done with some effort. Effort is needed between the observer and the object of observation. When there is effortlessness, when the mind does not function and returns to a natural state of calm, peace, this is freedom.

So, how to do it? There are different ways. Actually, to have freedom doesn't require any effort or method. You don't tread down the beaten track. You have to find your true nature, who you are. Before trying to know anything else, or follow any method—even those prescribed to you by the ancient saints— leave aside everything. Sit quietly and do not move your mind or intellect. Then observe the observer. This is your true nature, from where everything else comes. It is your own nature, don't forget.

If you make any effort or use any method of trying to achieve something at some distant future, this will bring you into time. And time is mind. So this will be the play of mind only. But your original nature is empty.

If you follow any thought that arises in your mind, you will find it arises from emptiness, from its source. And when you are aware, when you see "I am that source itself," then there is no need to practice anything. No need to go anywhere. And you will see that you have always been that. This is called *freedom,* and you are not to achieve or attain it in some distant future. It is already there. Any questions?

If one is aware that that is one's nature, when a concept of time or fear arises it's like a stumbling block.

This is a fear of facing emptiness, because you are living in so many concepts and things. When you meet the emptiness face to face, you lose everything: all the concepts of past, present, and future which you considered real . . . "This is my life." Are you holding on? This is your supposed strength. This is a feeling that you are living along with your concepts. When they leave you, you have fear. Fear of dying in the ocean of nectar. Fear of death in the nectar. What is the meaning of nectar? Eternity. Deathlessness.

We cling to something for safety, and we find we are holding onto the body, the mind, the senses, for safety. We don't realize that by getting rid of these things we have true peace. When we go from waking state to sleep, we lose everything that we held in the waking state. Relationships and possessions are lost to us in sleep. We have to let them go. We have no fear as we drop into sleep. We enjoy it, we welcome it. But we are afraid of this waking drop into emptiness because we haven't had the experience.

• • •

Papaji, you said that mind and objects are the same, that the objects cannot be there without the mind. Then it seems like a meditation practice, like Vipassana, that sets up looking at objects just reinforces mind.

By the mind, yes.

It is just more mind!

Like holding onto the tail of the dog.

So what can be the value?

This has a value. To allow you to raise this question is

enough value for it. Unless you hold the tail out straight, how will you know that it will return to crookedness? And that is the lesson from all the practices that are done. All the shastras and the scriptures say this is the teaching: "Reject us!" Even the descriptions: "Reject me!" This is the benefit you have been given. Otherwise you will not give up your concepts.

If you practice you will only become fatigued. When you are fatigued, you throw away everything. At that instant you are free. To get rid of everything is freedom. Everything that you do suggests "Get rid of me." To get rid of desires is freedom, freedom from the function of the mind.

The function of the mind is desire, so get rid of the desire. Get rid of the desire for samsara. Get rid of the desire to enjoy other worlds, like heavens. Get rid of that. Get rid of the creator of heaven and samsara. Get rid of him also. After that, get rid of this renunciation. Reject all of these; then renounce this renunciation itself. Then this is freedom.

Everything you do is only to get rid of desire. You enter an educational institution for studies. Eventually all the students reject this institution; they don't want to stay there all the time. After getting a degree, though the professors may be very good, you don't want to keep sitting there. You have entered only to reject it. Everything you do suggests "Get rid of us." Even the body will be happy when you get rid of it. All that you are doing is returning home, which is a very safe place.

And where there is no mind there is no form. Every thing, every time, even every breath wants to find and have peace. Even each inhalation needs rest for a moment. Before the exhale it takes a rest, in between. Nobody wants to work. Not even the breath wants to work. The breath enters emptiness for some time before entering again into functioning.

We must touch emptiness whatever we do. We can't do

without this empty moment. We ignore this moment because it is so readily available. You are not to do anything.

It happens between thought and thought also, when the mind takes a rest. Two thoughts cannot happen at the same time. Think. Stop. Next thought.

Always you are surrounded by that which you seek outside. You are inside that thing. And outside also; it is the same thing. Only we have to pay a little attention.

• • •

There has been a long-standing debate in the spiritual life. One view takes the relative approach of spiritual practice, developing oneself and gradually becoming enlightened, hopefully in the near future. The other view takes the position that spiritual practices are a distraction, which thereby miss the essence which is immediate. What are your comments on the relative approach?

By any tradition, I don't think the essence can be arrived at.

Do you mean that traditional forms serve to obscure the essence?

I don't think anyone living in the traditional way has been freed from samsara. Take the case of the Buddha. He rejected all the traditions. He tried all the traditions; he found they did not bring him the thing that he wanted. He tried, but then he said he could not arrive at the essence, at enlightenment. He sat under the tree and found the essence by himself. Abandon all traditional dharmas and you will arrive at the true dharma.

• • •

What is your comment on insight meditation?

The observer has to observe something, such as the breath. What you observe is through the mind. So whatever is gained through the observation is only mental. Who is the observer? The observer is not tackled, only the observed, the object of the senses.

One of the features of insight meditation is realizing that the observed is impermanent, unsatisfactory, and impersonal. There is a realization that nothing is worth clinging to. Through direct observation of objects, the person experiences real changes within, bringing peace, clarity, and contentment.

I think there is a clinging to inside through something that seems outside. Remove this wall of outside and inside. For example, nirvana is inside and samsara is outside, or form is inside and emptiness outside. If you are looking for emptiness, you are somewhere outside of it. So you construct a wall between you and something unknown. If you remove this wall, you don't need any meditation.

For insight meditation there are four objects of the mind: body, feelings, thought, and sense world objects. As you point out, there is no inquiry into the observer who seems to stand outside of all this. Where does the person go from here?

To whom does the body belong? To whom do the feelings belong? To whom do the thoughts belong? To whom do the objects belong? The body has no capacity to be enlightened because it is nothing but earth, air, fire, water. To arrive at freedom we reject the body. We also reject the feelings, thoughts, and objects. What happens if we reject all this? Who is capable of rejecting all these things? One is neither body, feelings, thoughts, nor objects. All this is due to Self. You can reject everything, but can you reject *I*?

What do you mean by rejection?

We all accept that we are in the waking state with body, feelings, thoughts, objects. Let us move towards the sleep state. In the last second before sleep, what do you do? Do you see all these things? What do you do to reject all these things and enter into sleep?

Nothing.

Unless one abandons everything one cannot sleep. How does one enter into sleep?

One is interested in falling asleep.

That may be, but you also have to reject all these things, even your wife who is next to you in bed. You love your wife, but still you reject her. Why do you reject all these beautiful things of life, and all this samsara?

Out of necessity.

Yes. If that is a necessity, what has happened when you go to sleep? Are you not more happy in deep sleep than in the daytime?

So the entering into sleep is the simultaneous rejection of the waking state.

We can agree on that. Then you enter this sleeping state that you do not know. What is there during the sleep? Who is awake? Are you happy or unhappy in deep sleep?

Very content.

He is very content. *(laughs)* In the supermarket we purchase many things. Is contentment going to yet another marketplace, or returning home?

Returning home.

The market is the body, feelings, thoughts, and objects. If all of these things could give us real contentment, we would never like to go to sleep. There is something more precious, and that is why we prefer to sleep. So in sleep we do not experience all of those things that we speak about. Who is awake during sleep?

Nobody that I know.

Something was awake. Because the next morning you say, "During my sleep I did not think about anything. I was very happy." So, during the sleep who experiences this happiness?

I have no idea.

(laughs) Excellent. Excellent.

There is the fading away of the objects—

Objects cannot fade out.

I appreciate that. This is just a form of language, not reality. Over the edge of the vastness of sleep, I cannot go.

Let us start from here. This waking state is samsara. Let us end body, feelings, thoughts, objects here. This ends, but deep sleep has not yet started.

This is the pure witness, pure sakshi. Meditators get stuck at this point.

Clinging occurs here. Beyond is unknown, beyond is emptiness. What is known is rejected, but beyond is not seen. Between that beyond (let us not give it a name) and things of waking condition, what do you see in this moment?

There is identification with I, which has an appearance of being solid and permanent.

This *I* and everything that goes with it comes to an end, but something beyond has not yet started. It cannot go back now. In this moment it is between the known and the unknown.

It seems that the thought is making a distinction between the known, called I, and the unknown. The thought that it must get rid of the known to taste the unknown, to taste emptiness. So the meditator continues practicing in the effort to end this I.

When this *I* is facing something else, this *I* will feel shy, like a new bride. You will be happy to be brought to this point, which is not easy to speak about with language. What is in front now is what *I* has never experienced in body, feelings, and so on. *I* is fatigued with all these things, and this *I* will simply disappear.

At this critical point is there a humility, a trust, that its own dissolution will take place?

It will embrace something else, which has no name. It is a jump into nectar with no subject and no object.

So, do you mean all the practices, meditations, traditions, and processes of "becoming" must be left behind, so a person can come to the edge?

If you give up all practices what will happen? If you have unloaded all the dharmas, you are absolutely naked. When you are naked you will jump into the ocean, never to return.

Seriously committed people wishing to leap into the ocean come to the edge. But then the person thinks, "If I drop my practice, my method, then I will just get lost again."

Yes, fear. That person who is not willing must be pushed.

Are you a pusher?

Some people need a push. You need a push to somewhere else where you are hesitating. But then one starts a tradition of pushing. You then need a son of God and a religion has started. Truly speaking you don't need a push.

Why not?

You are never at the end, and you never start from any-where else. Going to the end, to the edge, is a concept. It is only a concept of mind to think one has started from some-where else and is going to arrive, and that at this point you need a push. You have never started or ended anything, and you have never needed any push.

So we do not arrive at any critical point, or come from any-where?

There is no samsara and no nirvana.

So any construction of mind, such as being at the edge, is a complete fiction.

That is why it is called *mind. (laughs)* There is a suggestion of mind: "I want to be free from samsara." Then the practice starts, the method starts, and the dharmas start. To proceed towards nirvana from samsara is also a concept. Nirvana is a concept, another trap like samsara. But when we call it a trap, this is also a trap. We then want to get out of this trap. We know by a special spontaneous knowledge. Then you do not need any and do not jump anywhere, for there is no-where to go and nowhere to come from.

ng to be rejected and nothing to be accept everything and reject every-

• • •

I am a meditation teacher, but I am worried because I have not been sitting now for many months.

And what have you lost as you have not?

Nothing.

Sitting, standing, running—it doesn't make any difference. This has nothing to do with meditation. People who are crippled sit all the time. They are not meditating. And someone who is "meditating" whose mind is running toward sense objects is not meditating.

The fishing cranes are silent and concentrated and standing on one leg—what sadana—but they are finding fish! So it depends on the mind, and the mind will trouble you even while sitting, standing, sleeping. It will trouble you. You will worry that a cobra might be coming, that a tiger is coming. It will give you fear. Mind is trouble. Day and night it is never at rest. Even at night it is mostly dreaming. Very few minutes of real rest.

Even samadhi of yoga or practice is only another state. One day a yogi went to the king. He told the king that he could go into samadhi for forty days. For forty days he would not eat, speak, or even breathe. The king said, "If you can do this, I will give you a horse." This was what the yogi wanted, so he went into samadhi.

After forty days he did not come out. Years went by and the yogi stayed in deep samadhi. The king eventually died; the horse died. Still the yogi stayed in samadhi. The king's son was now on the throne, years later, and the yogi opened his eyes. He looked around and said, "I want my horse." This is only mind.

• • •

What is the meaning of dharma?

Dharma means *the way*. It has to do with concepts. The root is "that which you hold." Ways are different, different dharmas, different concepts. The highest dharma is to reject all dharmas. If you reject all concepts, all your ways, this is the dharma that will force you back to source. Otherwise, ways will take you from source to outside. When you reject all dharmas, this dharma will lead you home. Therefore, the best is the Supreme Dharma: to reject all dharma!

• • •

What about vasanas, latent tendencies or inherent tendencies?

These are the dormant habits inherited of the mind which are buried in memory. Accordingly, in certain circumstances they arise to grab the object. They return to memory, where they are again imbedded, and then appear again at proper circumstances.

After enlightenment, their power is destroyed because the identification is destroyed, the "doership" is not there. The viewpoint has changed. Interest is not there.

The viewpoint will be very stable and response to circumstances will be natural. Ignorant people carry the past and worry about the future. The jnani acts according to circumstances with no footprint in the memory.

What To Do

All doing has a goal. It starts in the past with a concept and projects into a fantasy of future. Doing can never take you anywhere you don't already know or can't conceive of. Trace the idea that starts the doing back to its root. There you will find the end of the journey that is never begun. Doing can never get you to that which you already are. Doing is moving away from that, not toward it.

Are there still desires after enlightenment?

Before enlightenment the desire must be for enlightenment. This is not a true desire but the attraction of the Self. In order for this desire to arise other desires must die. Ordinary desires must make way to create the space for the true desire of enlightenment.

After enlightenment, however, the Self-realized is beyond form, beyond the senses, and therefore not touched by the ordinary desires. After enlightenment the momentum of your desires may continue, but they do not touch the Self.

Once Krishna was down by the river on a holy day. The milkmaids all had offerings and wanted to cross the river to a temple on the other side. There was no boat and no bridge.

Krishna said, "Tell the river, 'If Krishna has never kissed a girl, then the river should part and make a path.' "

The women couldn't believe what Krishna was saying. It was said that he had 16,000 lovers. The river would never part! Krishna had kissed each of the women, so they doubted his words. But when they said to the river, "If Krishna has never kissed a woman, part for us," the river parted and created a dry path.

This is because the Self (Krishna represents the true Self) is immaculate and out of time. It has never kissed or been kissed.

• • •

I just came from seeing the Dalai Lama. He spoke of the problems of the world and the need for everyone to do right action. What is right action?

For an enlightened being there is no consideration of past or future. No consideration is given to the fruits of action. Rather, action is taken in each moment from emptiness. The fruits will take care of themselves.

The Dalai Lama was speaking to the common man who needs morality to guide his actions. Enlightened beings recognize that morality itself is empty, as is everything else. Therefore, right action, right speech, and the Buddha's eightfold path may come as a *consequence* of emptiness, but they will never *lead* to emptiness. Therefore, a seeker of truth looks for emptiness only, and everything else follows.

Then what practice do you recommend?

No practice. Let me give you an example. One day a dobi*

---

* *dobi*—washerman

was down by the river when a lion appeared to drink. A hunter in the bush shot the lion. He only wanted the skin. While skinning the lion, he pulled out a baby lion and left it on the bank.

The dobi took the baby and cared for it. The baby followed the dobi everywhere. When it grew big enough, the dobi put his washing on the young lion's back along with the donkeys. So the lion grew up carrying washing on its back and being treated like one of the donkeys.

One day a lion was hunting and came upon the donkeys grazing and eating grass. He couldn't believe his eyes. Along with the donkeys was a lion eating grass.

"How could this be?" thought the lion. "Donkey is natural, good food, and there is a lion eating grass!' So the lion jumped out of the bush and started towards the herd. All the donkeys started running. The tame lion ran also. He was afraid, just like the donkeys. The hunter lion chased and caught the tame lion. He jumped on him and knocked him to the grass.

The tame lion was very afraid. "Please, sir, please don't eat me," he said. "Let me go and join the others."

"But you are a lion," the one on top replied.

"No, sir, I am a donkey."

So the hunter lion took his charge back to the river.

"Look at your reflection," he said. "We are the same."

The lion looked into the water and saw two lions looking back.

"Now roar," said the lion.

And the other lion roared!

It's as simple as that. Don't practice being a lion. Roar!

But sir, how long does it take to realize? How long does the teaching take?

No time! How long does it take to roar? Open your mouth and it's finished.

• • •

I find myself doing less and less. The first week I was here I was so filled with the joy and love of your presence. Then that became a doing, a trying to recapture. Now I notice that if I am doing something, like watching my breath, or sitting straighter, I notice it and the doing stops, leaving me here in the present.

Both ideas, your doing something and not doing anything, both are impediments. Get rid of these impediments! It is not difficult. It is your nature.

If you don't do anything and give up the idea of doing anything, where do you return?

Right here.

So stay right here in this present instant. What doing or not doing is involved?

Yes. Or no. Both doing and non-doing or neither doing or not doing is involved. (Poonjaji laughs) *It is like a child's puzzle. Each way I turn is a trap.*

Whose trap is it? Who set this trap? "I want to do something" is a trap. "I want to do nothing" is another trap. This is your imagination only. Can you show me this trap?

Well, I think it is the idea of the doer who gets trapped.

Yes. So the doer is trapped inside. Finished! You are free

then.

When the idea of freedom arises in most people, instantly the thought arises: "What should I do to be free?" Then they watch their diet, their behaviors, their practice—all these traps. They run to some diet or some method or some practice.

Yet, if the desire for freedom arises, take a few seconds before you start to travel. Discover where you are going. If you are going from *here now*, then where are you going to?

Let me tell you a story. A team of mountain climbers was scaling Mt. Everest and they camped below the summit. Another team was returning from the top and saw them camped there. "Why are you camped?" they wanted to know.

"We are waiting for our map," they replied. "We forgot our map at the base camp and we have sent a Sherpa back to retrieve it. So we are waiting."

"But from here you do not need a map!" the returning team replied. "There are no avalanches, no problems. From here, *go straight to the top!* No map is necessary."

So drop all your maps and baggage. Go directly to the summit from here.

• • •

You say not to do anything, but some actions seem more in harmony with the Self and some seem to come from the mind. So isn't it important to do the right thing?

Spontaneous activity does not need to be manipulated by intellect, mind, or senses. Spontaneous activity will be conducted by a higher power *and it is not your concern!* If you are concerned, there is doership, and then karma and the world reappear. To become a doer—"I am doing"—you become responsible. But when you return to discover where this doership arises from, it will leave you. Then some unforeseen, indescribable activity will take charge of you. Unexplainable knowledge will take charge of you. Supreme activity, unheard of, will take charge of you. That is spontaneous activity within itself, and you are not in charge.

• • •

Accept what comes. Reject what goes. True renunciation is neither acceptance nor rejection.

There was once a sadhu who went to market. While he was gone his hut caught fire. His neighbors saved a few of his possessions from inside his hut and were getting buckets of water from the river and pouring them on the burning hut.

When the sadhu returned and saw them throwing water on the fire, he picked up his possessions that had been saved and threw them on the fire. His neighbors looked at him in disbelief.

Then it started to rain. The rain began to put the fire out, so the neighbors stopped the bucket brigade. At this point, the sadhu started carrying water from the river in buckets and pouring it on the hut.

Well, the neighbors couldn't believe their eyes. They asked him what he was doing. He replied, "When the fire comes, I welcome and assist it. When the rain comes, I welcome and assist *it.*"

So when a thought arises out of emptiness, do I reject the thought or the concept that it is holding?

If you are aware that the thought arises from emptiness, then this thought must be empty.

It feels like a wave arising in the ocean.

If it is the ocean, the ocean doesn't mind the waves. If there is ocean, there must be waves. These waves are samsara. Ocean is nirvana. All this is dancing.

No difference. Nothing to reject. How can you reject samsara? Where will you go? This is nirvana itself. Don't hold a dual concept that you have to reject it and go somewhere else, become a monk, change the color of your clothes, to get nirvana.

Instead, remove all colors that you have dyed the mind. Remove the mind from the clothes and that is all you have to do. Mind has to become a monk. Don't bother with the body and its clothes.

Mind is thoughts. Mind is ego. Same thing. Wherever there is name and form, this is ego.

• • •

Self will not complain that my mind goes to San Francisco, because San Francisco is situated within the Self itself. All thought processes are situated in and within the Self.

All your activities, all that you do–thinking, not thinking–all arise from the Self. No problem. The problem is when the ego takes the burden "I will do" and "I have done that." If you say "my Self has done—I have done that as the Self," there is no problem, and you will be 200% more efficient in your activity, even your day-to-day routine of life.

One can see the thoughts arising in the Self. California, San Francisco—these thoughts arise within the Self.

Yes, within the Self. It is not disturbing then, is it? When the waves arise in the ocean, is it a disturbance to the ocean?

So I should only think—

No. One should not think at all.

So these thoughts are the waves in the ocean, and we must remain in the ocean.

No, no! You are that! Why must you remain? You are that itself!

Yes. I have to establish myself in this.

No! No establishment either. You have to establish when you are something else. You are the Self. Now you are Doctor Boyle. Do you have to establish that you are Doctor Boyle?

OK. I'm the Self.

I AM is the Self.

I understand that I AM the Self. And that thoughts arising in me, the Self, are like waves in the sea. Nothing more or different. Thoughts like waves merge in the ocean. They come and they merge. All these thoughts will come and merge in me.

And the ocean will have no complaint. The ocean never says, "Why are they leaving me?"

I am quiet. I am always quiet.

Yes, very good. Trouble is only for the wave that will consider, "I am something different. I am not the ocean. My name is different, my form is different, my movements are different."

So the waves, out of their ego, think they are different?

This name and form itself is an ego. Wherever there is name and form, this is ego. And some falsehood. Some fraud. Wherever there is name and form there is some fraud.

• • •

What happens when we are responsible for others?

Responsibility will be executed by itself. This will be wiser because it is from the Supreme Power. Then everybody will be happier. But you do not trust this Supreme Power; instead you trust the ego.

What was the total time that you spent in Sri Ramanashram?

No time! When you are in love with anybody can you spend time in that atmosphere? This is the deepest bliss and you are never out of it. Time cannot enter there. Neither the mind nor the senses. Timeless instant. Then you will know that there is no time at all. Time is only ignorance. Millions and billions of years is an instant.

When you say there is no time and there never was, do you mean there is no separation from I AM?

I AM is I AM. *No time* is your natural state. When you

step out of this, you are instantly devoured by past, present, and future. This leads to all troubles, the many worlds, and it is all a trick of the mind. It is the mind that makes time.

When I am with the place where thoughts arise, there doesn't seem to be a particular place in the body where thoughts reside. Is this true?

No place either inside or outside the body. When you think "I am the body," then in the body it appears to reside.

I am still confused. Where do things arise when it is neither within or without?

Investigate *I*. *I* will go. Where do you automatically place this *I*?

On the body. Is this the conditioning of the past?

If you say "I will do it," but there is no attachment to the body, then where do you cling? There is no outside, no inside. You consider yourself the body, and therefore emptiness or consciousness appears to be confined to the body.

In Rip Van Winkle, a folk tale, the mind did not perceive time, but the body still aged.

All bodies age because the body is not the consciousness. The body is elements cooperating. When a man dies, the elements return. Even then you lose nothing. The elements are not destroyed; they simply return back to earth as the breath returns to air. So there should be no grieving over loss of body.

Only the fear of death is lost.

Is learning to see past lives helpful? People ask me to help them with this.

Why give them more trouble? One life is enough trouble. To help people you don't give them millions of other bodies. You don't possess the body; all this is mind only. All time is mind. Incarnations are from the body, not from awareness.

The ultimate Truth is that nothing has happened and nothing will ever happen! If you believe it or don't believe it, the Truth is not affected. If you know it from experience, it will help you to be happy.

As long as there is change, there must be something change-less to watch the changes. Without the screen there can't be pictures moving on it. The screen is changeless, the movie is ever-changing. Wherever there is change there must be a sub-stratum of changelessness. That is your own nature. On this, body, mind, and all phenomena are projected.

• • •

So even if you are realized, the body must finish its course.

It has to finish its course, yes. That is one way of thinking. Otherwise there is no course to finish. When the mind is acti-vated then you call it *a course*.

How does the manifested world exist for the enlightened being? Laws of nature and harmony, like the seasons, seem to exist in the waking but not in the dream state. I am confused about the differ-ence between waking and dream states. One seems more ordered than the other.

Looking for consistency is still looking to the mind. You have fixed the difference between the waking and dream state. But do not speak of one state while in another state.

If in the dream state you are hungry, how will food in the waking state help you? Do you want food cooked in the dream or waking state? In a dream state, if you see a friend, aren't you happy? And when a snake bites you in a dream, don't you suffer? Go to a dream doctor.

First realize, and then say which is order and which is disorder. It is most orderly to step into freedom.

• • •

The longer I stay here the more confused I get. I have the feeling that I don't understand anything anymore. I feel agitated inside. Everything is turning. I don't know what to do with that.

If you do not know what to do, then let it stay as it is.

I think something should happen.

Don't expect anything. Then it will happen. Don't have any expectations. Have you come here for expectations or to give up all expectations?

That's a good question.

I expect a good answer, too!

I think I have come here for expectations.

So are those expectations gone, or are you still carrying them on your head?

I'm confused about that. I don't know.

If you don't know then it's all right. If you don't know, then don't think of any expectations. If there are no expectations, then you are free. If you expect, then you are in bondage. Choose whatever you want. Expectations are never fulfilled.

But I see all these people having wonderful experiences here and I think I should also.

They have lost their expectations, therefore they have experiences. If you don't expect anything, then what is left?

Nothing.

Nothing. Then you will be happy. Giving up expectations is your nature. Not having expectations is your nature. Not expecting anything. No expectations is sahaj samadhi.

The Vehicle to Liberation

When people go on retreat to meditation practices it seems like something happens for people. There is a softening and calming.

Changes will happen.

Once I went to my master because abruptly all my practices left me. I was very awake.

In 1945, I was working in Madras and doing my daily practices which started at 2:30 a.m. and went until 9:30 a.m. Then I went to the office. One day the practices all left me abruptly. I simply did not wake up to attend to them.

In my neighborhood was a Ramakrishna mission and the swami called it "the dark night of the soul." He said, "You come to me and listen to my discourse every evening at 6 o'clock." Someone at the Vishnu sect, a swami, said, "You have to continue. Come to attend our kirta. Our guru says, 'Even if the vessel is clean you have to wash it for the next day.'"

I told him, "But if my cup is gold I need not wash. Maybe your cup is brass."

So everyone was telling me to continue practicing, you see. But I wasn't satisfied. Because my experience was that the practices left by themselves. I loved them. I was puzzled because I could not do them. I could not sit.

So I went to my master to solve this problem. I went on my Saturday holiday. I said, "I have been practicing for eighteen years, always meditating. I woke up and didn't want to sit. I am confused about what to do."

Then he asked me, "How did you come from Madras to Tiruvannamalai?"

I answered, "By train."

"And from the railway station to the ashram?"

"By horse cart."

"Where are these?"

I said I had left them at their stations. He said, "The means brought you to a place and you rejected the means. They left you. Means will bring you, introduce you, and turn back. You can't keep sitting on the train when the ride is over. The work of the practice has taken you to your destination; now get out at the station. The work of the practice is over now and you have to face yourself—a very pleasing situation."

You will be happy to give up the means. We are so attached to the means and in love with the means and enjoyments that we forget the purpose. To go somewhere you need the means. What means are needed when you are not to move? When you are at home you do not need any mode of transportation.

A real teacher will not give you anything to do. *No method. Nor can he give you freedom!* He simply removes the concept of bondage. You can do it yourself. If you can't, go to a good teacher. That is the teaching of a true teacher.

• • •

There once was a king who had no issue and wanted to adopt a son. He said to his minister, "Open the gate and let everyone come to see me between 8 and 6. When a man comes, arrange a bath and perfumes and then dress, then lunch and music and dancing. So when a man comes to see me he should be refreshed and relaxed and well dressed, so that I may adopt him as a son."

The gates were opened and everyone in the town came. People were taking baths and those fond of swimming were in the swimming pools. Others started picking up perfumes and bundling up the bottles to be carried home.

Then lunch started and everyone started bundling up boxes of food to take home. Next came the music and dancing.

Then it was 6 o'clock and the king said, "What happened? Nobody came to see me."

The minister replied, "We don't understand, Your Majesty. We opened the gates and everything was given. In the end, everyone left carrying bundles on their head to take back home." The purpose was forgotten along the way.

What is the purpose of human life? To return home. To meet the king. To get the throne. We forgot. And then at 6 o'clock the police come and throw you out. Time is over. If you go straight away to the king, all these things will be added onto you. They belong to you. Why don't you go and meet the king first? You don't have to bundle up all these things. These things belong to you. We forget the purpose of human life. You have to return and see the king. You start enjoying this thing and that thing and then the time will be over, the gates will be closed. So, it is time. And this time is this moment. So dress well, have a bath. Swim, wash, perfume yourself, eat well, and go to meet the king.

• • •

You say that although means get you somewhere they have to be rejected.

Yes. This is because when you really arrive you see that the means are totally useless, and your arrival was not the result of any means. When I saw the position after these means were rejected, I found these means had nothing to do with this situation. Once you have touched the philosopher's stone you cannot turn back to iron or brass, because you are pure gold. If means were involved you could reverse it.

We speak of means because otherwise no one understands. But once you experience you will see that means are of no use. Nothing touches it. Means mean mind. The mind is not responsible for leading you to that which is beyond the mind. Mind will lead, of course. These means will lead you to something related to mind. But going beyond the mind has nothing to do with means. And means belong to the past. When you speak of means it will take you to the past. To be as you are now at this very instant, what means are needed?

Choosing Samsara or Nirvana

You are afraid to cross the road to the other shore of freedom because you see a snake coiled in the middle of the road waiting for you. Each day you come back and see the snake and are afraid to continue. One day someone comes from the other side and says, "It is only a rope. There is no snake, only a rope." This authority tells you the truth, and you realize it. What doing is involved here? What did you do to the snake? Where did the snake go? "I am bound" is the same snake. The snake never existed. You must remove the impediments of fear and doubt. See the rope as it is.

Whenever there is duality, it is a dream state. Whenever you see multiplicity, you are in a dream state. Creator, creation, heaven, hell, or anything in between is a dream state. When you wake up, nothing ever existed. No gods, no creation, and nothing created. No world and nothing in it. That is total emptiness.

Then the first thought comes, "I am Katherine." In deep sleep nothing existed. No friends, no enemies. Nothing. In the morning when you wake up, instantly the first thought: "I am Katherine." Instantly, there begins the whole thing.

Time and karma appear with the first thought. So take this first thought, "I am so and so," and find out where it comes from. When you search, this thought will leave you and you will recognize who you are.

On this thought, "I am so-and-so," all other thoughts depend. The entire cosmos arises in relation to this thought. So take hold of this *I*-thought, the first thought. This *I* will vanish and leave you alone. This ego-*I* will help you to return back. Then you will know that nothing ever existed.

• • •

So you are saying we sometimes choose to see the illusion?

Yes. This is also illusion. *(laughs)*

When you become the seer, you see the illusion and then it does not exist. To see something you must look at it. To do this you must first separate yourself. This is the illusion.

So there really is only one desire?

One desire is no desire. How can you call it *one* without the concept of two? You cannot call it *one* unless there is something else. If you are seated all alone in a room and someone comes to see you, you may say, "Come in, nobody's here." Nobody's here, you say! One desire is no desire. It needs the support of the other desires to be one. When the others go, one is not there either. It is only from duality that we speak of oneness.

• • •

Why do I choose to believe the illusion?

You made the choice.

But why?

You made it. You can also reject it. You are satisfied with this illusion. You have relationship with this illusion. Therefore you believe it. If you made another choice, "I don't want illusion," then there is no illusion. It is your creation, your own imagination. The illusion does not exist.

And what do you mean by *illusion,* first of all? That which does not exist is called *illusion.* A mirage in the desert. It is your choice if you swim in it and proceed further. Your choice. And it will trouble you. If you proceed further toward the mirage in the desert and jump in to swim in it, whose choice is it?

You may never go swim in that river again. It doesn't exist. Only you choose it. And this wrong choice is called *samsara.*

To get out of this you must give rise to another choice. "I want to be free," also your choice. "I am in illusion," also your choice. So these two choices are there: whether you want nirvana or samsara. Choose one of these.

You chose samsara and now you do not see what is nirvana. Nirvana does not appear after you have chosen samsara. Once you have chosen samsara, you do not have the choice to be free of the desires of samsara. So you do not know whether nirvana exists. You were born here, you will stay here, you will die here. And this endless cycle will continue.

Someday you have to think wisely of what is good for you. Then you have to make a choice for something you have not seen. All these people of this world are lost in that choice which you also have inherited. You see all the people who have made the wrong choice, who are all going this way, believing someone else's choice! You are also going this way, believing someone else's choice.

Why is it that some kings have made this choice for freedom? Why did they leave their palaces and wives and treasure? Buddha was a prince himself and he made this choice. What problems did he have? He had a beautiful wife and son, all the luxuries of life. Why did he make this choice: "I want to be free"? He saw the suffering in the world. He had all the comforts and luxuries of life, elephants, a kingdom. Why did he make this choice?

It is the only choice.

If it is the only choice, why have so few chosen it? Why do we still follow the Buddha's choice 2,500 years later? Some lucky people inherit this other choice. You have different forefathers. You will inherit their choice. You have to shift your community, your involvements.

Which is the beneficial choice for you? You have been trying this one choice for millions of years, and you can continue to seek enjoyments there. There is no end to this. One day you make a choice of no more of these enjoyments that lead only to suffering.

I don't know how to go back.

Go back where?

Back into that freedom.

If you do not know, then you know it very well. Why did you come here and not go elsewhere?

There is nowhere else to go.

If there is nowhere else to go then this is a choice you have made. Yet you are still resisting, not accepting your own choice. You must honor the choice. You are very lucky to have this choice. You must honor it.

I do. But something is holding me back.

Only the desire must be there.

But what stops me?

You see some friends playing on the beach, and you want to join them to play in the sand.

I do not know the way.

There is no way. To be lost you must be somewhere else, not here. You must honor this choice. Once you glimpse the face of the true diamond, you must honor it by giving it its true value. You must give 100% value to it or lose it forever. Why forever? Because next time you will remember that you had this experience. Give it full value and do not depend on next time. If you compare, you lose it to the past. If you lose it, you lose it forever. So give it full value, full honor.

Are honoring and loving it the same thing?

Same thing. Enlightenment takes place in a finger snap. Here and now!—rarest of all. Nearer than your breath. Why postpone it for another hundred years? If something is most near, nearer than the breath, where do you have to go, what do you have to do to find it?

I got it!

Got it? Good! No effort is needed. Nothing to do. What is already here, very near, this is the honor. If you got it, you can never lose it. How can you lose what has no location, nearer than the breath?

• • •

It seems that each moment I can choose to be free. But is there another step when finally there is no choice? Are there different levels of freedom?

No. There aren't different levels of freedom, only different levels of the choices you make. Once only is enough to choose freedom. If you repeat it, it will lose its value. Hold onto the choice when it arises and march into that choice itself. Then it will become choiceless. Identify yourself with the choice. Immediately dive into it and then that choice will be no choice. Jump into this choice and become the choice itself.

Investigate where this choice comes from. Whose choice is it? This will lead you to choicelessness. When the choice is from the other side, there is no choice. From this side it is the choice of ego, who has fooled you for ages. One call from the other side is enough. The emperors have left their thrones, families, wives, and treasures. They gave full honor to this choice.

Leela

The waves are always washing against the shore. This is their movement and their noise. One day a little wave saw a large, old wave come rolling in from far away. The little wave asked the old wave, "Have you heard of the ocean? Is there really such a thing?"

The old wave replied with a crashing roar, "I too have heard talk of the ocean, but I have never seen it with my own eyes."

(Poonjaji looks around the room and smiles) The waves, their movement and sound, this is called *samsara*. This is the illusory separateness that causes suffering. Who here can describe the ocean?

My first day in satsang I looked out through a window. I could see birds. Those that were close passed by very quickly. Those that were far away, floating way up in the sky, took a long time to pass through my window. I realized that those birds are like my thoughts. I observed those thoughts until they didn't come anymore.

Now, out of my empty bliss, a thought is arising. I am ready for a new name. I realize that I was afraid to voice this thought. In observing this I see that all doubt and fear resides only in the mind. The bird of New Zealand is a Kiwi. It can't fly because it had no predators and therefore lost its fear. (he begins to cry)

In the night you came to me. I knew then it was time to give you a new name. Your name is *Dharma*. You are the first one to carry this teaching to the land of the Kiwis, as Bodidharma took Buddhism to China.

A thought is arising about emptiness.

Good! Now identify with that thought.

The thought comes from emptiness. If it is a thought about emptiness and you identify with that thought, this is pouring emptiness into emptiness. There will be no separation. And then the thought will return again to emptiness.

Now, if this thought of emptiness arises and you check that thought, this again is duality.

• • •

I stop people from dropping into samadhi in satsang. All samadhi has duration. The unchanging is ever-present. *Be it* in traffic with full presence!

I find myself needing to withdraw from social contact.

If you want to be a saint, there is a proscribed set of behaviors to cut off worldly sensations, and being a saint is acceptable here. Some sects go so far as to avoid eye contact with women, and the Nagas do sexual organ mutilation.

However, in my experience it is best not to change anything you are doing, as that will take care of itself. Emptiness is always alone and unchanging. It is now. Now itself is empty.

Just play your role in the Leela with no expectation or attachment.

• • •

Why do you come to me only in the waking state?

When the guru comes in what you call *the waking state* and wakes you up, it is only the dream state from which the guru is waking you.

Then what is the difference between the dream state and the waking state, in reference to the guru and waking up?

No difference. When you see a tiger come after you in the dream state, what happens?

I have fear and run and then wake up.

Likewise, in this so-called *waking state,* when you see the guru coming after you, what happens? No difference. When you wake up, you must have been sleeping. The guru tells you to wake up. If you don't wake up, you have not seen a tiger. You have seen a sheep.

There is no difference between an animal and someone who merely eats, sleeps, and has sex. Humankind, however, has the potential to want freedom from the whole process. The animal has no choice. You have the option to be free. You need not go to the slaughterhouse. You can avoid the slaughterhouse if you want to. Otherwise, you will be taken by the butcher, the king of death.

Right now you can avoid it. Death will take the body only. You have to know right now: "I am not the body. My body is in pain. My mind is not tranquil." Already it is separate from you. Whose body? Whose mind?

Always it is your true nature, the Self, the unknown which is responsible for the activity, but the ego claims it. When the sun is shining you say "I see." When the sun is gone you say "I can't see." Who is it who can see that you can't see? That I call *Self-nature,* through which seeing and not seeing is seen. You have to surrender to that supreme unknown emptiness and function from there.

• • •

Even though I feel so much peace and happiness being here, even being in emptiness, still the idea arises to do something. I feel it as a cloud.

No, it is not a cloud. It is a mist.

Even if thoughts come to do something, no problem. You can do 100%, while knowing absolutely that it is coming from the emptiness.

The sun shining, the clouds moving, all this comes from the emptiness. You will be more active, yet that acting will not disturb or trouble you, nor will it stupefy you.

There will be a role for you to play. Allow, and the activity will be there from the emptiness. Then this so-called *activity* will be empty.

I don't tell you to go to the monastery; instead, go on the battlefield and fight. This activity is equal to inactivity. Substratum is inactive, and you are that. Activity/inactivity has nothing to do with your status. Very spontaneous activity leaves no impression on memory. Samsara leaves footprints in memory. Your footprints will be like the bird flying. What you store in the memory is never-ending samsara.

If you know yourself, this baggage is destroyed. If you know yourself there has been no samsara at all. Not at that time, nor before, nor after. This is only imagination and the result of one thought: "I am the body." If you remove *the body* from the sentence what do you see?

To see samsara, you have to become the body first. Then time, and multiplied millions of bodies. Just imagination. When you wake up you will see that this is an instant of time. When you get freedom you will know this very well.

• • •

Nature is changing. Now, some people are concerned about nature and the planet. Many minds are working on the problems of pollution and the atmospheric changes. There are some spiritually minded people who even pray for the weather. What is all this?

This is also the working of nature.

No, it's the working of mind. I know that.

Yes. And where did you get this mind from?

I know. That is the mind.

Yes, it is the mind. But where did the mind get its power to work on this? Whose power did the mind get to work like this?

The Self, the source.

Yes. That source is called *nature.* If the mind is making some problems, it is also the nature working. Mind is also the nature.

Is the planet itself like a being?

The countless planets and solar systems hanging in space, this is all the creation of mind. Mind has tremendous power. You can do whatever you want. If you are not working towards freedom, the mind can show you that path also, if you want to make use of it. Mind is pushing you. If you say "I want freedom," this is the association with the mind, and the push of the mind only. Mind wants to be peaceful, so why don't you have friendship with mind itself?

Friendship?

Mind is your friend and also your enemy. You can use it as you like. As you wish, so will it happen. As you wish, so will you become.

But medicine has the power to heal the body, and that is not mind.

That is mind with a capital *M*. It is the mind which likes to reach to the Mind. The direction of the mind is to the Mind itself and that Mind is absolute.

Thought is within the mind itself. When it returns to the mind, it is a quiet mind, an ocean without waves. And when the waves rise from mind they become the universe.

Is Satan the mind?

The evil power of the mind is the demon. This is also a reality within the realm of mind. Mind has an evil tendency and that tendency is manifested as a demon. In Sarnath one of the temples shows paintings of the Buddha sitting under the Bodhi tree. All the temptations are shown. Armies with javelins are coming to attack him, to keep him from enlightenment. These are the stored-up tendencies of mind rising up, your own tendencies, your own creation. When there is no mind, no universe, no god, when you quiet the mind, all phenomena end.

How do you quiet the mind?

By looking at it. Look at it and it will be quiet. Then it will be objectified. Some subject must be there to look at this object. Then you are separate from what you are looking at. Discover whose mind is agitated or whose mind is at peace.

When you say "Whose mind?" it's one of the best jokes I ever heard.

Yes. You are joking and so I am joking. When you say "My mind is agitated," you joke, so I joke.

• • •

I have heard you mention Leela. *What do you mean?*

What is Leela? Leela is like going to a movie. First there is the screen, and it is blank. The light is shining on the screen and it is clear light. Then the projector starts and the movie appears on the screen. People marry and die and love and fight and then the movie is over. The screen is again blank. The actors all the while know they are actors. No one is born, no one dies. The actor plays a king, but all the while he knows he is an actor.

After realizing emptiness, is there still preference and taste?

Yes, but it is empty. It is only the role of the king or the slave who has the taste. As soon as you identify with the role, as soon as you believe the movie is real, this is samsara.

• • •

Once a king was out hunting all night. He came home the next morning and his guru was waiting up for him. The king said to the guru, "First I will take a short rest."

In a little while he woke up and said, "Guruji, I have a question. I just had a wink of sleep. During this sleep I was a beggar. One day I was going to the village to beg and many other beggars were there. But they were all going in the other direction. I was going to town, but they were all leaving.

"One of these beggars said, 'Where are you going? Today is the birthday of the king. Come with us and the king will give us clothes and great food and money.' I went with them and was fed and given new clothes. I decided that today I would bathe and put on the clothes the king gave me, and today I would eat like a king.

"While I was bathing a dog ran off with my food. I chased this dog with a stick. I got the food back from the dog and then I woke up. In this instant I was a beggar who had come to beg from the king on my own birthday! Guruji, tell me which is true. In that moment, was I a king or a beggar?"

The guru replied, "Both are dreams. In this instant we are in a sleep state as well. The entire world is sleeping. Sleeping means begging. Everybody is begging something else. Kings are begging. Everyone is begging."

Now you have to wake up, while everyone else is sleeping.

Whoever stays in the Self, thinking of the Self, speaking of the Self, is in a true waking state. And when you forget it, "I am not the Self—I need something else," this is a sleep state, and then you chase the dog for food.

Desire

What is the difference between my will and God's will?

You are imposing your will on the god. You say, "Let Thy will be done"; you really mean, "Let my will be done." You are telling God, "Let my will be done." God has no will because he has no desire. So, really, it is "Let my desire be done." Who is it that imposes this will on God? God has no will. This is your will, your desire. God doesn't say, "Let my will be done." When it is fulfilled it will be your own will fulfilled. God in heaven is not your attendant.

What is the will?

Desire only. Without desire where is the will? You can actually utilize your will only once. That one time is the will to freedom. "I want freedom. I want to be free." Use your will only for this purpose. Then all will is fulfilled. Otherwise it is no use using your will to chase this thing and that thing.

Why don't people want enlightenment?

Because the mind engages them in the enjoyment of the senses. And they fear giving up the pleasure of the senses. You can count on your fingers the number of people who truly want to be free.

Everyone is afraid: "I will lose the world, my attachments, my relationships, my dear ones." This is a foolish concept. On the contrary, when you are enlightened you will begin to have really good relationships, even with the animals, even with plant life. You will love everyone. First enlightenment, then you will be a good human being.

What pushes us to want freedom?

Good luck. A mountain of merits are accumulated, then you will want to be free. If you miss in this life, you will carry over to the next life until there is a mountain of merit.

What would you tell someone who does not have the desire for freedom? How can they accumulate merit?

Those people don't come to me. If you are looking for diamonds, do you go to a potato shop?

Aren't merits involved with time and therefore the mind?

Yes. When you cross beyond, then I will speak to you in a different language. No merits or demerits or gods or practice.

So is merit related to worthiness of the soul?

All these things are only in the scheme of ignorance. Really there are no merits, no demerits, no bondage, no enlightenment, and no search for enlightenment. This is the ultimate truth. If you agree to this, then I will speak on this matter.

You come for freedom; in truth there is no difference between bondage and freedom. If you want to be free, this is from the viewpoint of bondage. When you are ready to reject both bondage and freedom, this is the Freedom I speak about.

There is no merit, no practice, no gods, no sadana. True meditation for freedom is pure, immaculate. No thought of freedom may enter. And this meditation is over in seconds. As long as the concept of freedom is there, you are bound. Do not have any concept, not even that you are meditating. When I see someone meditating like this I wake them up.

Are you saying that meditation for freedom is itself bondage?

Yes. When you run to the idea to meditate for freedom, where are you standing? In bondage or not? Do you not have an idea in the mind that you wish to be free from something? So you sit in bondage. You are meditating on bondage, not freedom!

This freedom you are looking for is the opposite of bondage. True freedom has no opposite. So start your meditation sitting on freedom itself. Have freedom in your hand and then what are you meditating for?

Nothing.

Ah, that's it. How do you know it is nothing? It has no name, no form, no concept. Meditate on that, within that, for that. OK? It cannot be conceived or achieved or attained. *(much laughter)* Transcend this thought of freedom. Then freedom won't be there. Knowledge won't be there. *(more laughter)*

What happens to the senses?

First you experience. First attain that state and then report. You are asking, "After I marry, will I have a son?" Why don't you ask, "After I marry, what happens when I am fifty?" Why not ask me that? First experience. First have the wedding. Then you will know everything.

What happens to the senses when you are sleeping, to begin with? When you are sleeping, there are no senses, there is no mind, no worry, nothing. This is the sleep which is still ignorance. The mind grows tired and relaxes and you give up everything. For four or five hours the mind temporarily relaxes and lets go.

And you have a thought to wake up tomorrow at 6 o'clock. With this thought you tie a rope, and then enter sleep. "Tomorrow I will do this thing and that thing." And that rope you tie around your head to wake you up tomorrow. Sleep is where you lose everything. But that sleep is filled with awareness. You are quite aware during that sleep. Now you discover.

• • •

I can't will myself to change. You can't will yourself not to have desires, because that is more of the ego, isn't it?

This will cannot be rejected so easily. This will, "I want to be free"—let's call it *the last will,* the last desire for the highest thing which is perfection, eternity, emptiness—it cannot be rejected. It will take you somewhere and then it will vanish. This desire will burn itself out, and what will remain is your nature. So be thankful for this will. Very few lucky people will choose this freedom. Cling firmly to this desire, and it will take you to freedom and then vanish. Every desire needs the support of another desire. Otherwise, one desire is no desire. Therefore, it is freedom itself. There the means and ends are the same. Intense desire for freedom alone, allowing no other desire to rise, is freedom itself.

Once you consciously know you are free, desires will rise, but they will not have a ground, because these will be roasted seeds. They will not have sprouted in the memory. You will already know the end.

All desires actually end in freedom. Your desire is fulfilled and you are empty. The emptiness brings you happiness, but it is unconscious. You attribute your happiness to a possession, not the emptiness. It is the freedom from desire that gives you happiness.

All attraction is Self to Self. No body can give you happiness. It is not the body, not the meat that gives you happiness. It is Self to Self. Attraction is Self to Self. This is the secret. Once you know it, there will be only love in the world. Hatred cannot be there.

Only an instant is required for this recognition. Once only. Just a moment. Look into and recognize yourself within this instant. You don't need a long program spread over years to recognize this freedom. You are already free. It is only recognition that isn't there, that you are postponing. You must recognize your own nature or you will not be happy.

• • •

Lately the desire for freedom has grown. I feel a fire and strong desire for freedom, so strong I can barely stand it. It has intensified and burns inside so much I can hardly stand it. This desire for liberation is flaming inside. I cannot postpone it. I must have it now. I want to know immediately. Desire still burns.

When this desire itself is burnt out, then there will be freedom. You must give more intensity to this desire—much more—so that it may be consumed in its own fire, resulting in freedom.

How does it become more intensified?

When there is no support whatsoever for any other desire.

By the removal of all other desires?

Only the desire for liberation, with no association of any other desire. When there is no other desire except liberation, how can you call it a desire? If there is even one other desire, then you can call the desire for liberation a desire. Where there are no other desires left, how can you call it a desire at all?

I don't know.

You must know. Put yourself in that situation.

I still don't understand.

If there is only one desire left, without the concept of the second thing, or second desire, how can there remain one in the absence of the second? Where are the limits of this one if it is not defined in relation to something else? When there is no second, this desire will also go away, and then *that* will be freedom.

This desire for freedom is not going to win you anything.

It will disappear, that's all. Otherwise you would have to achieve something or attain something. Then you would lose it, and then it would not be your nature. Your nature is not to have any desire.

The desire doesn't seem to be on an object, it seems to be on the Self.

This desire arises from within the Self to attain the Self. It will return to where it arises from. It will go back. It will not take you from this place to somewhere else to be fulfilled. This desire will disappear. If you don't even give rise to this desire for freedom, what will be left?

I don't know. It has always been there.

Don't give rise to it and then see, what is the situation?

No desire then? Not even the desire for freedom?

Yes. *(pause)* Now, what is this? What is left?

First, all desires vanished, and this desire for freedom was left. When this desire for freedom also left, what remained was freedom.

When you say *freedom,* is there any desire for freedom now?

No.

What happens now?

No desires.

So stay as this! What trouble is there if you stay like this? What would you call this situation: bondage or freedom?

Neither.

Yes, very good. When you say neither bondage nor freedom, in between them both now, give rise to desire. Then I will see what we will do. What desire comes? What thought comes? What object comes? What subject is left?

Nothing.

Very good! Very wise man.

• • •

If there is any method, it is to reject everything that can be rejected. When you have rejected everything that can be rejected, what is left is yourself. You can never reject yourself. Can you say, "I am not I"? Being cannot be rejected; all that can be rejected is becoming. What you become can be rejected. But Being, which is empty, which is nature, which is source—how can you reject the emptiness? Can it be rejected? If it is something, it can be rejected. But if it is empty of all things, empty of all ideas, how can it be rejected? Now you have to recognize, "I am this."

So when a desire arises, should we reject this desire?

No, don't reject it. Find its source. Turn back to where the desire originates; find it and you will find the source of all desire. If you have to meditate, do it this way. Investigate and discover the source of this desire. Where does your desire to meditate come from?

Dissatisfaction.

Where does this dissatisfaction come from? Go back to where it comes from. Does it come from the world?

No.

OK, so reject outside. This dissatisfaction came from inside. Return to this inward source of dissatisfaction.

It came from my mind.

Where does the mind come from? You said "my mind." Whose mind? Find the source of mind. Satisfaction and dissatisfaction are in the mind, right?

Yes.

So find the source of the mind, which is sometimes satisfied and sometimes dissatisfied. Now trace the source of the mind. Go back to where it comes from, now.

• • •

It seems like the desire to be free is like the queen ant of all desires. You can spend forever going after all the little ants, or just go after the queen ant and that is the end of the ant colony.

(laughing) Yes, yes. Looking for the source of the mind, or "I want to be free," there is no difference. The desire for freedom is the same process of returning to the source.

When you were searching for the source of mind, which other desires trespassed?

The desire to come up with something. The desire to really know. I feel like I know the words.

Reject the words, including the word *mind* itself. What you were asked to do is to return to the source of mind.

I find quiet.

OK. Before, you said "dissatisfaction." In this quietness do you find dissatisfaction?

Not in the quiet itself.

So, when you return to the source of the mind, you find quietness. Who is quiet?

I am.

Then stay here and tell me if you see dissatisfaction anywhere around. "I am" you said. So question to *I* and question to *am* to find any dissatisfaction. These two are left: *I* and *am*. So let the *I* question the *am* and the *am* question the *I* to see if there is any dissatisfaction. Who is dissatisfied?

When they question each other they are not dissatisfied.

OK. Reject one of these now. Reject *I* or reject *am.* We are still tracing the source, you see.

I reject am.

Excellent. Just the *I* is left then, so question to this *I,* "Who are you?" *I* questions *I.* "Who am I?" There is no second left, so let this *I* question itself. You say, "I am Bill." Do you ask anyone else, "Am I Bill?" Who is Bill? Where am I?

Nothing.

Nothing. So even this *I* vanishes here. The word *I* disappears. When there is nothing to question, you can reject even *I,* OK? What is left now? Go beyond where the *I* arises. Do it quickly. No thinking. You are very close. Don't miss this moment.

(long pause)

OK. When you say "I," what do you see? Any name? Any form?

In I, *no.*

No name, no form. That is your nature. Will you recognize it now? Will you discharge into it?

If you can't speak, it doesn't matter. I am satisfied. Only stay as such and keep quiet. Honor this situation by keeping quiet and becoming quietness itself. When you are quietness itself, then try to jump out of this quietness. Where will you go?

• • •

I've been feeling so much energy and bliss. You said bliss is also to be moved through.

Bliss is the last sheath to reject. In bliss there is still an activity of someone enjoying something else. Separation. Most people get stuck here. They find some happiness or bliss and they cling fast to it and don't go beyond.

I sometimes feel so much energy when I am with you that I can't even hear what you are saying. When you said "Go beyond bliss," I started crying and crying.

This energy is not different from the source. This energy is responsible for the sun shining, for the wind blowing, for you meditating. The problem is when you attribute this energy to something else; maybe physical, mental, intellectual, vital, or blissful. Through this energy itself we feel happy, we breathe; this is the undercurrent. When you understand, there is nothing to do about it. Only shout a roar, *"I am this energy!"*

There are moments when I feel that I am this energy. Then other times the mind says I must do something.

Even then this energy is with you. "I am doing" you say, but what is the energy that lets you do? I lift a hand; what makes the hand lift? What is this undercurrent? We don't recognize it because it has no name or form. What makes the mind meditate? That is called *emptiness.*

You don't need any method, any practice, any concept, any book. Any way, any thing, any practice will take you away from that. Any *doing* will take you away from it, not towards it.

Look for the silence. What is it? Where does it come from? How do you differ from that silence?

Anything that appears is not true. In the desert you see a river mirage and you are thirsty. The more you chase it, the further away it moves. You can never quench your thirst in that river. This is samsara. You want to quench your thirst and you move toward an object of enjoyment and you get no enjoyment. Once you know, by your experience, that it is only a mirage, that no river exists, this understanding alone is enough. You will not run after these things. You will stay where you are.

This is the rise of desire, to quench the thirst running after a mirage. And nobody is happy running after imaginary rivers in the desert. Nobody is happy. One desire leads to another desire. Who is there that says, "I am satisfied"?

So we have to turn to that which is beyond suffering and misery. All the appearances are not true. They were not there before the beginning, and they will not be there after the end. When a desire is fulfilled, for a moment you are happy. If you watch closely, you will see it is not the object that gives you happiness. In that moment there is no desire, and your mind is empty. This emptiness gives you happiness.

There is no difference between desire and samsara. No desire, no samsara. The whole world is chasing the fulfillment of desires. When you've had some experience, after some time, you will not desire anything. That perfect state is called *light wisdom*. The desire for freedom itself must be abandoned. This is the last desire. Then you will cross to somewhere else. You will recognize that you are everything. Then what can you desire?

Master, by your grace, I've noticed all desires are gone. I didn't do anything. They just left.

Desires don't exist. If you touch that point of who you are, you are fullness itself. What can you desire?

Only to come back to see you.

Realization

Everybody knows very well the direction that has been said and heard and known. I want to take you in the direction that has been unheard, unsmelled, unsaid, unthought. No mind has ever entered there. The mind retreats after facing the light. The shock, what you call *fear,* is this fear. Taking off is a fear. Once you take off you can't return to the same runway. Where are you going to land? If you know, tell me.

You have launched us into space and left us there.

(laughs) You can't abide. Don't cling, even to the emptiness. You can never touch any port. Because you left everything behind. What is unthought, unseen, unimaginable, this I call *emptiness.* Take off from the emptiness itself. Emptiness is a concept. Freedom is a concept. Enlightenment is a concept. They have brought you from other concepts such as "I am suffering, I am bound." You have to accept concepts of freedom and emptiness. I advise you to take off from there, from freedom, from enlightenment, from any concept of whatever it is. Nobody has seen tomorrow. This instant is the time. Don't postpone this instant for the next day.

• • •

After we talked I felt much emotion and a very powerful long-ing for freedom. Then I felt that all the world wants freedom, that everyone yearns for it. It was a relief to recognize that it is not just about me, but that I am just an expression of that.

Yes, excellent. We are all returning to our source and it is not an individual question. All the beings of this planet are only you. This thought of freedom is consolidated, belonging to everybody. If one individual frees himself, all have been freed. How do you explain this?

Supposing you sleep and during the dream there are many, many people who are aspiring to liberation. They are doing different exercises and practices. You are telling them what freedom is. You are speaking to everybody. Meanwhile some-one asks you how to attain freedom.

He questions you about it, and instantly you wake up while speaking about freedom. When you wake up from this dream of others aspiring to freedom, what happens to those you left behind?

They have returned to the source.

When you woke up you did not leave anyone behind, bound. This is only the imagination that we are bound. All are free. Who is not free? When people are bound they are sleep-ing, and they are all projected on you. In the dream there are all those people aspiring to and working for freedom. When you wake up, where are the others?

It is a fact. Very difficult to understand, but a fact. Nobody is bound and truly speaking, none created. None has been created. Everybody is in the source and is free. Nothing and no one is out of the source. Where can they run to get out of the source to be free?

• • •

Who is journeying for freedom? The one who is already free. Just get rid of the concept, "I am the body, separate from the source." You return to what you always were. This journey will take you back to your home. It will not push you to any new kind of dimension. You cannot become or get what you are not. You have to be what you already are.

When you wake up from the dream, nothing else existed! Where there is name and form, there is still dreaming. Where there is name and form, there is fraud, not reality. In waking state there is no difference between man and man and birds and rocks, all total being.

When you aspire to freedom, the whole cosmos is with you. Keeping free of any thought is the best way to help the world when the world is crying for peace.

• • •

Papaji, will you say a few words about why, when a man receives the grace, he becomes outspoken like a lion, completely unbound, calling a spade a spade?

There remains no fear of limitation. Anything you were involved in was bound by beginning, middle, and end. When you transcend, it is boundless, beyond the frontiers of the mind. Now there is no fear. Now you can respond fearlessly. You respond spontaneously from moment to moment. There is no imagination of the future. You are living in the present, which is living free. If, however, you are related to persons or things, and you are afraid of losing something, this is bondage.

When you say that fear is about losing what has never been gained, I don't understand.

Fear is always of the past. Someone once challenged this and said, "When I leave here, if I see a policeman I am afraid. The fear is in this instant, and is therefore a present fear."

But I say this policeman was already settled in memory. Seeing this policeman, you went back to the policeman in memory who did something to scare you. That policeman from the past became this policeman.

Also, while the fear is in this moment, it is fear about the next moment. Will the policeman come and get me? This is now the future, based on the past. There is no difference between past and future. The foundation of the future is the past.

When we speak of living in this present moment it has nothing to do with the present that is related to past and future. But we have no other word. So don't hold onto the word *present* either. The concept of present must also be transcended.

Transcend name and form. Transcend the light also. Only then will you transcend the present itself.

• • •

Time is mind. Fear is time. Whenever there is fear, there is time. What we are speaking of is neither time nor mind nor fear. You never touch time, you never touch mind, you never touch fear. Fear is only in duality. Where there are two there is fear. When you are yourself, there is no fear and you are *aloneness.* You never touch anything else. Time doesn't touch, mind doesn't touch, fear doesn't touch. You are beyond all that.

All these are concepts. Fear is removed by understanding. Duality is removed by the wisdom of unity. Duality is only in dreaming. When you wake up, nothing else existed. That is total freedom.

This instant of time is beyond the concept of time. Therefore, questions disappear. That is your home, your final abode, where nothing appears. Nothing can touch it.

This is the knowledge of the unknown which is empty. Nothing is there. No wants, no needs, no desire. This is peace. This is your own Self.

You don't have to attain it, achieve it, or acquire it by any method whatsoever described by any man or any god or any creator. No effort is needed to reach there. It is the easiest of all to know who you are. You don't need to travel to find freedom. You are already free.

• • •

Anything that can be rejected, reject it, including this sentence. What's left?

Do not accept any word or speech. All my words are fingers pointing to that unknown which I cannot describe. Reject my words and you will see what is there for you to see.

• • •

I find myself getting caught in the greed that I've missed something, that there is something more I haven't got.

This greed is welcome. It will not cling to any object. It is greedy only to measure the fathomlessness. This engagement could be carried on up to the end of your life span and you will be happy to do this. Not seeking, but intention for deeper peace. This can be kept and there is no problem. You can't get out of this. Always the engagement will remain. This is peace itself.

When you have true peace, you will desire to see if there is even deeper peace. This is Selfward, not outward. You will always like to love more, if you get involved with this love. It is an unending search in the direction of the unknowable.

I don't advise you to stop it. This activity is in the direction of inactivity. It is activity within inactivity. Only joy will be there—beginning, middle, and end. This joy is your nature. It is not searching for something else.

The Guru

What is the relationship to the man who shows you the rope?

This is the finger pointing at the moon. If you only see the finger, you will miss the moon.

Sometimes there is a desire to have the man walk along with us to point out the snakes and ropes.

You must go alone. All alone. No one can do it for you. This way is not a beaten track where you can be led by some- one else. You don't need any help and there is no track. All beaten tracks are the past. Do away with all tracks, all paths, and have no one to lead. All tracks are merely imagination of past and future. Remove all imagination of past and future and where do you stay?

• • •

What about all these gurus that do harm?

Yes. There are two sects. How many sheep, how many goats, how many pigs and water buffalo do you see? That is one sect. And how many lions have you seen on your trip here in India? That is the other sect. As long as there are sheep, there will be herders. How many lions do you see being herded?

• • •

Is obedience to the teacher a way of dealing with ego and personal desire?

Yes. The tradition prescribes that. To ward away the ego you have to have obedience to the teacher. And this teacher is none other than your own Self. You have to be obedient to that which you are seeking.

However, A TRUE TEACHER DOES NOT EXPECT OBEDIENCE FROM ANYBODY!

If you have ego, it has to be brought down to surrender to a higher authority. If you have no ego, there is no need to be obedient to anybody. If you need help erasing this monster, you must turn to a higher authority to take care of this ego. If you have no ego, you need no teacher. The teacher must be your own Self.

But when you ask this question, I think you refer to some preacher, not teacher. A teacher is one who is enlightened himself, and enables another to be enlightened. If there is a candle, it has a flame, and any other candle that touches this flame will be enlightened, just like the candle it touches. If a teacher doesn't give you enlightenment, he is a preacher, not a teacher.

It is so difficult to find a teacher these days. There are mostly preachers. A real teacher has no teaching. He merely apprises you of the fact that you are no different from himself, the Self! You are already that! What is there to teach? The teacher tells you that you are already that. A teacher should be able to allow you to know that you are that itself and not seek anything anywhere. You are already that! You are already free! The ultimate truth is that there is no teacher, no teaching, and no student.

• • •

Within this dream of differences, why do some people seem to have the power to transmit the Self-nature and others don't?

Difference from whose side? From the one who transmits or the one who receives the transmission?

When I come here, I sit with you and feel something. When people sit with me they may not feel anything.

The man to whom this power of transmission is attributed is empty. His mind is empty. Where there is fire there is naturally heat. But fire does not know it is hot. People go near the man with the empty mind and their desire will be fulfilled. He may not know. If he knows, it will not be done. Only in the man who has no desire will the desire be fulfilled.

• • •

You speak of a razor's edge. We can't really slip off this razor's edge; it is actually just an idea, isn't it?

The sharpest idea! Very narrow. Two cannot walk abreast. If you lose balance you will be cut. If you walk on the razor's edge, you should be single-minded. Not between two minds. And if you stop you will be cut. This is the direction that will lead you to nowhere. This is an idea and here two ideas cannot travel. Then the idea of the sharp razor goes away when it has done its job. This will lead you to immortality.

Welcome the decision to walk on this, throwing all other ideas away. Who will walk on this edge? Very few.

The razor's edge is not to give rise to a thought. This is the razor's edge. Walk and see. Thoughtlessness will lead you to emptiness. Not by understanding or argument, but by *being* it, throwing yourself into emptiness—nothing short of it. Not understanding or conception, but by jumping into emptiness right now! When you jump into this, you cannot but speak the Truth. Instantly you are free. Don't postpone this freedom, and don't make any plans for the future; then it will happen. Planning is a trick of the mind. The thought arises, "I will make a retreat and do it there." Time means postponement.

• • •

What happens when the guru dies?

The guru never dies. The guru is your own Self within. You seek him outside, and therefore out of grace the Self takes form and manifests as "the guru outside" just to tell you, "I am within you." That is the whole point of a guru. Trust yourself and look within. Guru is that which dispels darkness. The word itself means "that which dispels darkness, one who dispels ignorance."

There are times when I see that we are part of the same continuum.

Yes. That is being. Not seeing. Being. There is no difference.

I wonder why I become afraid when I am feeling so much love.

Fear of too much joy, happiness, freedom, which you have not tasted before. It is a strange taste, a strange kind of love/beauty you have not seen or heard before. Therefore, with a new environment the mind is not comfortable and returns back. That is called *closing*. But it brings some taste along with it. Even if the heart seems closed, that taste is quite enough. If you know your heart seems closed, it is really open. If it were closed you would not see that it seems closed. It is in the opening of the heart that you say, "My heart seems closed." You mean, "Previously my heart was closed."

The thought persists that a free being would have a soft, open feeling all the time.

Closing and opening require a door. There is no door. Only imagination. Look and see if there is a door or lock. If there is no door, how can it be closed?

Fear or thinking is the door.

Yes. Imagination, not reality. How do you remove the imaginary door? Nobody can tell you. There is no way. This is your own imagination.

What about the sensation of tightness?

In the evening you see a snake. In seeing a snake how does the fear arise in the mind? How do you get rid of the fear? You find a stick or a rock to hit the snake, or you take out a pistol to shoot the snake, isn't that so? All these things will come up on seeing the snake. From the other side a man comes and says, "What are you doing? Why are you waiting? It is only a rope."

So look at the snake—fear, safety, stick, pistol, stone, movement has stopped. You are not going forward. A man tells you it is a rope. How does the heart open? How has the fear gone? How has the snake disappeared?

When the habit occurs of contraction or knotting, then there is the thought, "No, I don't want a knot." Then the thought arises that freedom is not complete because of a sense of inside and outside.

Some like to keep that thought up to the last when the body drops. Freedom is freedom now or when the body drops. Liberation here and now or after the fall of the body, it is the same. Don't prolong it.

• • •

Each day of satsang with you is like lifetimes of bliss.

Let me tell you what *satsang* means. *Sangha* is association. *Sat* is Self. So, *satsang* is Self-association. Your association with the Self is the ultimate satsang.

If you do not recognize where the Self is for this association, then find a teacher who is Self-realized. This is the next best to your own.

Keep quiet. Nothing to think. Silence. Just be quiet. In quietness, in silence, the Self arises by itself. This is the best satsang. If you have no confidence in your own Self, then you seek someone. And by chance, if you are honest, if you are sincere and serious, this Self will lead you to some other place where you will meet the very same Self who will tell you, "I am your own Self."

• • •

Many gurus tell their devotees that they must surrender. Often people give up their jobs and surrender to the guru. They know they are in a dream world and they want to surrender to something greater than the dream.

This is forced on people by shepherds.

Shepherds?

Shepherds are the leaders of religion. Shepherds herd all the sheep. Only the sheep are herded, not the lions.

Some spiritual teachers put out a strong message that seekers must surrender, let go, and follow the master.

This creates much fuss when shepherds say, "Come to me, I will give you rest." This kind of surrender is not worth believing in. It has benefited no one yet. Every instance of time for millions of years is a thought. This instance of time is empty. Nothing exists and yet nothing is nonexistent. It is this emptiness that I speak of again and again.

What is surrender?

Teachers misinterpret surrender. Surrender is abandoning

the concept that "I am bound." This is surrender. When surrender replaces the concept "I am bound," then nothing can
be said of what is surrendered to.

• • •

We have been comfortable in limitation, so we don't touch
limitlessness. When someone imposes limitedness on us, we
readily agree. Anything you desire to achieve is a limitation.
And you don't have to desire limitlessness, because that you
already are.

You make frontiers. The idea, "I need freedom," constructs
a wall between you and freedom. Remove the concept that
there is a wall between you and freedom and what happens?
This wall is imagination. You don't have to remove the rubbish
of the wall. What happens if you remove this wall, which does
not even exist?

You haven't removed anything.

Then who were you, who are you, and who would you be?

• • •

*Poonjaji has the reputation of being very strongly affirmative
about people's experiences. Is it valuable to be very affirmative to
the person who is tasting of something?*

When I respond I am absolutely empty. I don't search for
an answer to the question. I am just empty, without thought.
Unconcerned with what is going on. The answer comes from
emptiness and not from Poonja. Poonja then has no substance.

This student is not my concern. The question is not asked to Poonja. To whom is the question addressed? Poonja cannot bestow freedom upon anybody. The question is asked to the unknown.

This is the teaching of non-teaching.

Yes, this is the teaching of non-teaching. The rest is preaching. The teacher has no teaching of his own. The teacher is pushed to speak and has no responsibility for what is spoken. Simply, you live as a free man, an immaculate, empty man. This is the best teaching that one has to give somebody. Sit absolutely quiet. No thought. This teaching is the best teaching, which no one can reject and all can benefit from.

• • •

Master, I have just returned to your feet after one month away. I know all of this is a dream and that there is no real leaving. So why do I feel such joy, bliss, and overflowing love to be back in your presence?

We are sitting here at the bank of the Ganga. You see her rushing and noisy as she streams past, running always to the sea. And at the Bay of Bengal the sea comes up to meet her. The sea comes up and takes the form of the Ganga. And they mix. And who can say which is which? And then all is silent.

I have to thank you so very much.

Why thank me? What have I given you? If we give each

other something, then we thank each other.

It is all so clear. Now I can see it.

Now you can see it. You have not taken my eyes to see. The eyes are yours, and sight also is yours.

The fear is gone. The fear is gone. The fear to speak is also gone.

Ah.

It was already on my lips a few times. Then there is no question any more.

Excellent. Good. Thank you.

You have freed us from so many things.

Yes. *Your* things.
I am happy. All of you are going home victorious. All these years I was going to your door. Now I am eighty years old and not able to go. So I am sorry I have given you the trouble to come here.

• • •

Is it true that you made the statement, "After I die I will leave the teaching with no footholds to hold onto"?

Why wait until after I die? *(laughs)*

Just as a bird leaves no trail in the sky as it flies, the true teaching leaves no trace in memory. The teaching must have no teacher and no student. If the teaching comes from the past or memory or concept, it is *preaching* not teaching. This teaching never was. *(he smiles and looks around the room)* It never will be. *(he pauses and then laughs)* And it never is.

About Sri Poonjaji

The Secret of Arunachala was written by Abashiktananda, a Catholic priest who spent many years living in India. The following account of Sri Poonjaji and his teaching was recorded in 1953, and is excerpted in whole from The Secret of Arunachala.

The first time that I met Harilal was in the cave of Arutpal Tirtham on a Friday, March 13.*

It was about four in the afternoon. I was sitting on my stone seat outside the cave, when I saw two men coming towards me along the narrow passage which lay between my cave and Lakshmi Devi's little house. They introduced themselves and sat down beside me. One of them was a Tamilian, but it soon became clear that he was only there to accompany the other, perhaps merely to help him in finding my hiding place on the side of the mountain. The other was a brahmin from Panjab, who now lived in the South, either at Madras or Mysore—I was not clear which. His family had been left behind somewhere in Uttar Pradesh, in the Gangetic plain. He himself had known the Maharshi extremely well and had also lived near him for a long time. He had now come to Tiruvannamalai for two days and was staying near the ashram in an annex of Dr. Syed's bungalow.

* This was in 1953. *Harilal* is a psuedonum.

This was about two miles away from my hermitage and meant using tracks which were often difficult going. I therefore asked: "How did you manage to get here? Who can have told you about me? Who directed you to my cave?"

"*You* called me," he replied, looking me straight in the eye; "and here I am."

At this I gave a rather skeptical smile, but he continued in all seriousness: "Let me say it again: It was you who called me. The Self attracts the Self. What else do you expect?"

We spoke about the Maharshi, his teaching and his disciples, with all of which he was perfectly familiar.

Near me lay some books, including the Bhagavad-Gita and the Upanishads, from which I liked to quote to my visitors. This was because of my experience in the previous year of a brahmin pendant from Tanjore who only abandoned his lofty airs after I had recited in one breath the names of the principal Upanishads. At that time, I had not yet received the forceful lesson of the *avadhuta* of Tirthamalai!

As our conversation passed from the subject of the Maharshi to that of the Scriptures, I picked up one of my books to quote a text from it, for I did not possess an Indian's memory which enables him to learn everything by heart. I added that I had begun to learn a little Sanskrit so as to be better able to understand these texts.

"And what is the use of all that?" asked Harilal bluntly. "All your books, all the time lost in learning different languages! Which language do you use to converse with the Atman?"

As I attempted to defend my point of view, he cut in again: "Forget about it! In fact, apart from the Atman, what else is there? So your English, Sanskrit and the rest, how do they benefit you? Are they any use for conversing with the Atman, with the Self, for speaking to *yourself*? None of that leads anywhere useful. The Atman has nothing to do either with books, or with languages, or with any Scripture whatever. *It is*—and that's all!

"I also," he continued, "was mad about reading once; but I never learned anything from it. Now I read nothing, or so little as makes no difference. Not even the Gita, whose words in the old days were all the time ringing like music in my heart. I don't meditate any more either—the Atman is nothing to do with mediation. It is the same with *japa,* the repetition of divine names, with mantras, litanies, bhajans, every kind of devout prayer and lyric. At one time I quite naturally made use of all these—and with great fervor! Of course, I used them with my children, and still do on occasion; but only for their sake, because at their age they need such things. It is rather like the way I join in their games; after all, is it not all just play, the *lila* of the Atman, the Self?"

I had certainly never before met an advaitin who was so sincere and authentic. There are indeed crowds of people in India who talk learnedly about advaita, especially in the South and in ashram circles; but they are generally the first to run to the temples to offer pujas for the success of their ventures on the stock exchange or to obtain some promotion; not to mention the terrible ego-centeredness which so often accompanies the intellectual profession of Vedanta. Even so, surely Harilal was going too far? Ought one not take account of individual weaknesses; and so long as one has not yet realized the Self, it is unreasonable to act as if one had. I had discussed this one day with a well-known professor of philosophy at Madras,* himself a faithful disciple of the Maharshi, a man who was absolutely convinced at the rational level of the truth of

---

* Dr. T.M.P. Hahadevan

advaita, and moreover one who had real experience of the spiritual life. Nevertheless, he had remained completely faithful to his ceremonial duties, often visited temples and offered in them the customary pujas. In his view, one should not give up these outward rites until one has ceased to be aware of duality (between oneself and the Self). When I expressed surprise at this and reminded him of the teaching of Sri Ramana, he was willing to go so far as to say that as the time of the "crossing over" approached, when worship and prayer become somewhat artificial, and even unnatural, then—with the guru's approval, of course—one might abstain. I therefore reacted pretty vigorously to Harilal's remarks.

"Who realizes, or has realized the Self?" he replied. "That is all a matter of words. The Atman cannot be reached. Apart from the Self, what else is there? Who reaches the Self, except the Self? 'Non-realization' is simply an excuse that one gives for trying to escape from the Real, and continuing to lead with a clear conscience a stunted life of prayers, devotions, and even asceticism, all no doubt very satisfying to the little ego but in fact utterly useless. Has the sun really set, merely because I have closed the shutters? The fundamental obstacle to realization is precisely the notion that this realization is still awaited.

"Of course," he conceded, "reading is not to be entirely rejected. It is better to read than to daydream or gossip. And meditation is better than reading. However it is only in the ultimate silence that the Atman is revealed, if one may so speak. But once again, we have to guard carefully against supposing that this silence has anything to do with either thinking about it or not thinking about it. For the Atman cannot be reduced to anything capable of being said, thought or taught, or equally to the negation or absence of thought."

Then I said, "What about all these peddlers of advaita who

haunt the streets and public places of our country, and flood the libraries with their publications? They protest as loudly as possible against those who propagate Western religions, and yet they themselves are more narrow-minded than any of their opponents. They 'possess' the truth, and anyone who does not accept their supposedly all-inclusive Vedantic viewpoint is in their eyes merely a fool or a fanatic."

"You are perfectly right," replied Harilal. "As soon as advaita is presented as a religion, it ceases to be advaita. The Truth has no 'Church.' The Truth is the Truth, and it cannot be passed on to others by anyone at all. The Truth has no need of anyone's help for its propagation. The Truth shines with its own light. He who claims to possess the truth, or says that he has received it or that he can hand it on, is either stupid or a charlatan."

He went on questioning me about myself, my way of living, and how I understood the spiritual life.

"Even among our own people," he said at last, "I have met few like you."

Then he turned to his companion. "Please do us the favour of leaving us by ourselves for a moment; we have to discuss certain matters together."

After the Tamilian had moved away, he continued: "There is only one thing you need, and that is to break the last bonds that are holding you back. You are quite ready for it. Leave off your prayers, your worship, your contemplation of this or that. Realize that *you are. Tat tvam asi*—you are That!

"You call yourself a Christian; but that is meaningless at the stage you have reached. Look here, listen to this—it is I who am the Christian, and you are the Hindu. For anyone who has seen the Real, there is neither Christian, Hindu, Buddhist or Muslim. There is only the Atman, and nothing can either bind or limit or qualify the Atman.

"Now tell me about your spiritual experience."

Once again I attempted a smile to hide my emotion, as I asked: "How do you want me to tell you this?"

But he was not smiling. "At all costs I must know. Tell me however you like, with words or without, but you must tell me."

We were sitting on the stone seat with legs crossed, facing each other. I made no reply. As the silence deepened, I closed my eyes, as he also did, and we remained like that for a long time. Then I opened my eyes and he opened his, and for some seconds we gazed at each other. Once more our eyes closed, and when finally I looked again, I saw that his eyes were wide open, but as if unseeing.

"You are a lover of silence," he said.

"It was you who suggested my using it for answering your question. That is why I did."

"You have done so remarkably well. Now I understand everything. You are quite ready. What are you waiting for?"

"Ready for what? Alas, I feel myself so feeble when before God I recall what I ought to be."

"Enough of this nonsense! Stop talking about differences. There are no differences anywhere. There is only the Atman. God is the Atman, the Self of all that is. I am the Atman. *You* are the Atman. Only the Self exists in itself and in all."

"But how do you know that I am ready?"

"When a woman is ready to give birth, of course she is aware of it. And every woman who has already been a mother knows the signs without a shadow of doubt. It is the same with those who are near to the awakening, or rather, whose *I* is on the point of disappearing in the light of the essential and unique I. I saw it in your eyes this morning when we passed each other in the bazaar without you noticing; that is when you called me."

"You are speaking as if you had been sent here expressly to give me this news."

"Whether I was sent or not, I had to say this to you. Now it is done. If you do not believe me, that's your affair. But you can't get out of it. If necessary, we shall meet again for the final decision. Or perhaps someone else will intervene, someone you will be unable to resist."

"But if, as you say, I am so near to the awakening, why do you not go ahead and awaken me?"

"There is no question of awakening anyone at all. Who indeed is the sleeper? How could one awaken that which does not sleep and has never fallen asleep? Sleeping, dreaming, being awakened, all that is a matter of the body and the senses which are located in the body, including of course thoughts, desires and will. Are you this body? Are you this thought which you have of being or existing within the limits of this body? When you are in deep sleep, do you still have any thought or awareness that you are? But still, even then, you exist, you *are*. You are in truth neither this body which sleeps or alternatively keeps awake, nor this thinking mind, sometimes clear and sometimes confused, which wanders about, constantly picking up impressions on every side, nor are you even the personal awareness that you have, beyond all these thoughts, of being—an awareness which vanishes in deep sleep, in coma and at the dissolution of the body.

"It is through you that that is seen and heard, that it is thought and willed. You are what remains when nothing is any more seen or thought, willed or heard. That is the Atman, the Self; it is what *you are* yourself in reality and beyond all outward appearances which change and pass away. *Tat tvam asi—*

You are That! What prevents you from realizing this?

"Can you remember the time when you were born? Can you discover in your memory some moment which would have been the first moment of your existence? Have you any awareness of beginning to exist? Did you not exist already, well before the time when you can remember that you existed? If your being is tied to the memory that you have of it, then what happened to you in the times of which you have no recollection? What happens to you at the moment when consciousness goes to sleep?

"Let me tell you again, there is only one thing that you lack. Enter into the *guha,* the cave of your heart, and there realize that *you are!*'

"The cave of my heart!" I cried. "I indeed try to remain there as much as I can. And to be living in a cave on this mountain is for me a most valuable help in that attempt. In this cave where I am living—and still more, in the further cave where there is no light at all, where I withdraw for meditation—I have been given an indescribable peace and joy."

"Your rock cave is a dead thing. How can it give you peace and happiness? It has nothing to do with the joy which you say that you feel when you withdraw into it. Rather it is you, you in your own depths, who are the supreme peace and joy. It is you who fill your cave with that peace and joy which you yourself essentially are, in the cave of your heart. The bliss, *ananda,* of which you experience a kind of echo—are you really so simple-minded as to think that it is this rock that bestows it so generously upon you? How can you indulge in such dreams and refuse to *see?* In fact, you neither give nor receive anything whatever, least of all this peace *(shanti)* and this joy *(ananda).* You are *ananda,* pure *ananda;* and this *ananda* cannot even be called *ananda* any longer, for it cannot be seen, or conceived or named. It simply is."

As I led Harilal towards the path which led down from the mountain, I pointed out to him the magnificent landscape which was spread out before us—near at hand, the town of Tiruvannamalai with its Temple; and in the distance, the countryside with rocky hillocks jutting up among the fields and stretches of moorland. Just at that moment the sun was setting. I was telling him something about the splendor of its rising each morning, immediately facing my cave.

"I have no doubt that it is a glorious sight," he replied; "but can it be compared to the dawn of the Self, to the rising of Being?"

• • •

In the following year* we met again, Harilal and I, in our beloved Tiruvannamalai. This time I was staying with a friend in a house near the ashram. It was there one evening, sitting on the flat roof in the light of the moon, that he told me his story.

He was born in western Punjab, the part which was torn away from India in 1947 and was the scene of so many atrocities at that time. His mother was the younger sister of a sage who at the beginning of the century was very well known as Ramatirtha and spent his last years among the Himalayas. When he felt that the hour for the great departure had come, although he was only about thirty years of age, he simply went down into the Ganga and "disappeared," not far from Tehri.

Harilal joined the army as an officer. However, he soon wearied of a calling which allowed him neither the time nor the freedom of spirit that were necessary for the pious practices to which he had been accustomed since his earliest childhood.

* 1954

Since his earliest years, the thought of God was what, more than anything else, possessed his soul. He was only about six or seven years old when he went off about twenty kilometers into the jungle to look for some sadhus who had opened an ashram there; when his parents finally discovered him, he gave them this answer, without of course having any idea that it was an echo of the Gospel: "Why come to look for me, instead of leaving me with God?" His devotion to Krishna became so intense as he grew older that it bordered on hysteria. He went so far as to wear women's clothing so that Krishna might take him for his beloved Radha and might take pity on him and show him his face. Everywhere he went he repeated the name of his lord; and if in the street he happened to hear the adorable name, he had to use every ounce of his strength to prevent himself from falling down in ecstasy in the middle of the crowd. Obviously it was quite impossible for him as a soldier to keep up his life of prayer, meditation and *puja;* in addition, it was wartime, and discipline was naturally very strict.

He asked to be relieved of his duties. His superiors pointed out to him the madness of such a request, as his reports were excellent, his promotion assured and a splendid career lay before him. In fact, his companions, all young officers in those days, were to fill the highest posts in the Indian army after 1947. However, he stood his ground, and explained his reasons to his commanding officer, who finally understood the position, supported his request and saw that his resignation was accepted.

When he returned home, his father gave him an unsympathetic welcome. He was already married and had three young children. How was he going to bring them up if he refused to make his career? He himself had in fact never wanted the marriage; but since it was the tradition and his father wanted it, and since, in any case, apart from his passion for Krishna, he was perfectly indifferent about everything else, he allowed it to happen.

Only his mother understood him, and he certainly needed the support of her affection to get through that difficult period. At the same time, he devoted himself more fervently than ever to his pious practices with a view to obtaining Krishna's *darshan*. Whenever he heard mention of some "saint" visiting the neighborhood, he used at once to run and throw himself at his feet, beseeching him to enable him to "see God." Likewise to the sadhus who came to the house begging for a little food he would address the unchanging request, but alas, always in vain.

One morning he happened to be sitting in the veranda of the house, when a sadhu appeared who had the complexion and bearing of a South Indian. Harilal brought him some fruit and asked him to be seated while waiting for his mother to prepare the food.

"Swamiji, I have a desire to see God," Harilal said to him. "To that end, I have left my career in the army, and so incurred my father's wrath. I pass my time in reciting mantras, signing bhajans, and offering puja; I wait on the 'saints' with whole-hearted devotion. I have asked goodness knows how many mahatmas for the secret of obtaining the *darshan* of Krishna, but it was always in vain. None of them could help me. Krishna seems to care nothing for my distress and shows me no pity at all. Do you yourself by any chance know of anyone who would be able to make me see God?"

"Certainly," replied the sadhu without the least hesitation. "Go and see Ramana, and all your desires will be fulfilled."

"Where is he to be found?" asked Harilal, leaping up, "so that I can run to see him immediately?"

"He lives in South India, at Tiruvannamalai, one night's

journey by train from Madras. Don't waste a moment. Your hopes will be more than fulfilled."

Harilal at once noted down the name, the address, the place and the way to get there; then he informed his family that he was setting off for Tamilnadu.

His father took it badly. "What about your wife and children? Is this how you understand your duty? Was it not enough to leave the army, that you must now rush off to the other end of India, indulging your mad search for spiritual adventures?"

But the Lord is kind to those who hope in him. The very next day a friend showed him in the newspaper a totally unforeseen offer of employment at Madras, which suited him exactly. He borrowed three hundred rupees and set off.

Some days later he dismounted from the train in Tiruvannamalai Station. Like all pilgrims, he hired a bullock-cart to carry him the three or four kilometers which separated the station from the ashram.

He found the Maharshi seated on his couch in the little, unimpressive hall with its tinsel decorations, where at that time he lived with his disciples. Harilal bowed to him and sat down; after some time, evidently gripped by some strong emotion, he went outside. He would not speak to anyone, but merely asked the time of the next train to Madras and ordered a bullock-cart to take him to the station.

He was already seated in the cart, when someone stopped him. "How is it that you are leaving already? You have only just arrived!"

"I am not interested in so-called sadhus, who make fun of people," he replied sharply.

His questioner looked at him with bewilderment.

"Yes," Harilal went on; "your Bhagavan, I have seen him

just two weeks ago in my own home in the Panjab near Peshawar. I myself gave him *bhiksha*. I asked him if he knew anyone who could open my eyes and make me see God. He had the nerve to send me to this place, more than three thousand kilometers from my home. If he was really able to make me see Krishna, why couldn't he have used his miraculous powers up there, in our house, or at least in the jungle nearby? But let that be. I arrived here, but he did not speak a word to me, or show a single sign of recognition. It would not be so bad if he was a real 'saint'; but there is no sign of a rosary round his neck or in his hand. During the whole hour that I have spent in front of him, not once did I see him telling his *tulasi* beads, not once have I heard him murmur the names of Krishna or Radha. He is a complete charlatan. What is the use of staying here any longer?"

"What!" replied the other; "you must be dreaming. Ramana came from Madurai to Tiruvannamalai forty-odd years ago, and everyone knows that he has never once left this place."

"But even so, I have seen him myself, with my own eyes, in my father's house in the Punjab, at the beginning of this month!"

"Two weeks ago, Bhagavan was here. You can ask anyone you like in the ashram. Listen to me; be reasonable. After making a journey like yours there is no sense in going away after half a day. You don't have to hurry. Stay here and rest for at least two or three days. Then you can see. Now come with me and I will introduce you to the *sarvadhikari*, Swami Niranjanananda."

Harilal no longer felt able to understand a thing—Had he been dreaming then? Was he dreaming now?—but he allowed himself to be persuaded, paid off the driver and stayed at the ashram.

He spent several days there, then returned to Madras to take up his duties. In Madras he so arranged his time that he could devote the greatest possible number of hours to his devotional exercises. On the other hand, he went back every week, or at least every fortnight to Tiruvannamalai, for clearly the Maharshi was making an ever deeper impression on him.

One day he was in his puja-room, engaged in singing or praying before the picture of his beloved Krishna, when suddenly he found Ramana at his side.

"If you want to see Krishna, take this mantra and use it constantly," he seemed to hear him saying; and a mantra was whispered in his ear.

He at once repeated the mantra and began to recite it habitually. However, he still had some doubts, and so on the following Sunday he appeared at Tiruvannamalai.

"Bhagavan, was it really you who came to teach me this mantra?" As was his wont, the Maharshi's only reply was an indistinct Hmmm-hmmm.

"Bhagavan, should I go on using it?"

"If your heart tells you to . . ."

As Harilal told me, after this he set himself to repeat the famous mantra with such diligence and fervor that he even took to running away when he saw anyone coming up to speak to him, such was his fear of allowing his lips to stop even for a moment the recital of the formula on which all his hopes depended.

At last, one day the miracle happened. Whenever Harilal spoke of it, one could not help seeing how his eyes still shone with the joy which that marvellous vision had brought. Krishna was there in front of him, "as truly present as you are before me at this moment"—a lad of about fifteen, whose body, whose smile, no words of ours could possibly describe.

"And in my soul I experienced a joy," he added, "such as I had never, never felt before."

His lifelong hope was now realized. At long last, Krishna had come to him.

On his next visit to Tiruvannamalai, Harilal prostrated before the Maharshi with deep feeling.

"By your grace, Bhagavan, I have seen Krishna!"

"Oh! So Krishna came then?"

"Yes, he came and graciously revealed himself to me. What bliss!"

"Then he went away?"

"Yes, of course," replied Harilal, somewhat surprised.

"Oh, oh!" was all that Ramana would say, but he smiled.

Harilal continued to repeat his mantra and to offer his customary worship to Krishna with even greater fervor than before. Who knew? Perhaps one day Krishna might come again!

And, indeed, once again in the same place, while he was offering flowers and incense to Krishna, Harilal beheld a figure standing before him. But what had happened? He did not see Krishna with his flute, or even Radha, Krishna's beloved! Before him was Rama, bow in hand, accompanied by Lakshmana!

Harilal was utterly at a loss. He consulted the most learned swamis in Madras, but none of them could explain why it was Rama that came, when all the time he had been inviting and calling upon Krishna. He did not want to have anything to do with Rama; it was Krishna alone who enthralled him. So why should Krishna play with him in this way and make fun of him?

As soon as he could, he returned to Tiruvannamalai.

"Bhagavan, can you explain what has just happened to me?" Then he told him the whole story.

Ramana simply smiled, and said gently: "Krishna came to visit you and then went away. Rama has done the same. Why are you concerned with gods who come and go?

"Don't you see, japa, mantras, puja, prayer and ritual are all excellent up to a certain point. But the time comes when all that has to be left aside. You have to take a leap into the beyond . . . in the beyond you find the Real. Only when everything has been left behind, devas along with everything else, can you find the vision which has no beginning and no ending, the vision of Being, of the Self."

When Harilal stood up, the devotee of Krishna was no more. In the depth of his heart there was now shining the vision "which neither comes nor goes for ever." He had desired to see God; and God had finally revealed himself so near to him that henceforth it was impossible ever again to address him as "Thou," for the unique Light was now shining in his own deepest center.

• • •

Later on, I often met Harilal. We understood each other so well and were so deeply in agreement that we could not fail to use every occasion that was offered of being together and speaking of those things which were central in our lives, especially as we both found that there were so few people with whom we were able to discuss them.

Even so, Harilal found it very difficult to understand why I should still feel myself bound by the ritual and other obligations of my Christian faith. "The Atman, the Self, is bound by nothing," he often said.

But it also set him a problem, as he well knew that it was

neither laziness nor dishonesty that held me back from taking the final step into freedom, for which he believed I was "entirely ready" . . . *

I particularly enjoyed meeting him in the jungles of Mysore when he was working there. Each time I passed through that part of the world, for example, on my way to Poona or Bombay, I always broke my journey for a few days at least so as to see him.

After his "conversion," as he had already told me, he stayed in South India to be near his guru. He left his wife and children in the north, having settled them in Lucknow to escape the massacres of 1947. For his part, his only object in working was to supply the needs of his family and to pay for his children's education. He often told me how joyfully he would quit working, once his son was married and settled in his turn. Meanwhile, his children came every year to Tiruvannamalai during their holidays, and Sri Ramana took great pleasure in playing with them—times which for them were unforgettable.

He was in charge of some iron and manganese mines deep in the jungle and far away from towns, which could only be reached by appalling roads. He lived in a hut made of straw, close to his workers. It was certainly a marvellous solitude for anyone who could do without human society, but it was one that his other colleagues had little liking for, as they did not know the secret of living in the depths of their being. As far as he was concerned, he joyfully contrasted his present lot with that which would have been his, supposing in his passion for Krishna he had not escaped from the army and so renounced

---

*In fact, Abhishiktananas's attachment to Christ and to the Church remained unbroken until his death in 1973. In his journal under 28 December 1971 he wrote: "If I say that I believe in Christ, that means that Christ is God for me. God-for-me, because there is no abstract God . . . Jesus is God's face turned towards man and Man's face turned towards God."

all prospects of wealth and honor.

Since hearing those very simple words from Ramana which had changed his life, he had found that all his desires had completely died away. Nevertheless, he applied himself to his work with complete efficiency, and spared no trouble to make his mines as productive as possible and also to discover new and even better deposits of ore. Anyone seeing him striding round in his long boots as he surveyed his mines, or else taking the wheel of a jeep or truck, could with difficulty have guessed the secret of his deep inner life. He especially liked describing the surprise of a young German who had heard about him and came looking for a sadhu whom he expected to find either naked or dressed in rags, seated motionless in some cave or else hidden in some jungle thicket.

There were some, however, who "recognized" him, even though they were still unable to penetrate his secret. Some came to realize that he was near them, although they had not even heard of him previously, and then wrote to him, inviting him to "return," this time in his bodily form. There was also a brahmin doctor in North Kannada, in whose outhouse he had taken refuge one day during a sudden storm, booted and muddy, wearing a black leather jacket. On that particular day, they happened to be observing a festival in honor of their absent guru. Harilal was invited to share in the meal, and despite his objections, his unsuitable clothing and their complete ignorance about his caste, he found himself placed in the seat of honor and treated as their guru. Later this same family built him a room in their village, in the hope that he would consent to come there from time to time and give them his *darshan*.

There were also unforeseeable meetings, the result of insignificant details in various people's programmes, but which occurred just at the very moment when his spiritual help was required; skeptical Westerners would say "pure chance!" but in India people speak more reasonably of the *leela* of the Self at work in complete freedom among those whose ego has vanished. I will only tell one story to illustrate his power of intuition. One morning at Rishikesh he was already seated in the Bardinath bus together with some friends from Lucknow and Gonda. Suddenly, he got down, made his friends do likewise, and removed his luggage. The other passengers thought he was out of his mind and told him so, especially a sadhu who had a seat near his. Ten hours later, this same bus crashed into a ravine from a height of two hundred meters.

From time to time he returned to Tiruvannamalai, though much less frequently after the Maharshi was gone. It was on one of these occasions that we "found" each other—"the self calling the self!"

He went almost every year to Lucknow to see his family and also the numerous friends who looked forward to his coming. His small room was practically always crowded, as his son Surendra told me one day when I also was passing by.

He never indulged his visitors and was merciless towards those who clung to visions, ecstasies and other such "mystical" phenomena. He was hardest of all on those who in his view were misleading people, by letting them halt at the outward practices of religion, though these may be as comforting for the disciple as they are often profitable for the so-called guru.

One evening a well-known doctor stopped his car in the narrow lane which ran past his house.

"They tell me, sir, that you are the possessor if *siddhis* [spiritual powers]. Is this so? I desire to see God; can you help me to do this?"

"Why not?" replied Harilal calmly.

"Then . . . ?"

"Then, if you have honestly made up your mind, we can see about it. But I shall request you to think about it first very seriously. This is not a trifling matter, and it may lead you much further than you suppose."

"No matter. You need not worry." Then, with a knowing smile, he added: "I am quite able to pay for it, you know."

"Really," said Harilal; "in that case, let us put our cards on the table and talk business."

"How much do you want?" As he said this, his visitor took his cheque book out of his pocket and laid it on the table.

"How much are you ready to pay?" was Harilal's frigid reply.

"If you were to ask me for one lakh [one hundred thousand rupees], then I would write you a check for it immediately."

"You really could spend one lakh on this business? Would that not put you into difficulty? Give the matter a little further thought before deciding. In round figures, how in fact are you placed?"

The gentleman began to do some sums. Property, house, securities, bank balances, all together he had at his disposal between sixty-five and seventy lakhs.

"I see," said Harilal grimly. "Are you by any chance pulling my leg? You say that you wish to see God, that this is your supreme desire, etc. And you are only prepared to give up for this object the sixty-fifth part of your possessions. You cannot trifle like that with God! You have made me waste your time and also mine. There is no point in your staying a moment longer. Good night!"

• • •

Glossary

ADVAITAN - Follower of Advaita teaching (non-duality).

AVADHUTA - A self-realized saint living outside society's customs.

ANANDA - Pure conceptionless bliss.

BHAKTA - Devotee.

BHAKTI - Devotion.

BHIKSHA - Offering of food to the guru.

BODHISATTVA - A being whose life is dedicated to the enlightenment of all beings.

DHARMA - Truth/path.

DARSHAN - Grace of the self.

ENNEAGRAM OF CHARACTER FIXATION - A system for describing the structure of the ego.

JNANI - An enlightened one who knows through direct experience.

KALPAS - Cosmic circles of time. Four 5,000-year cycles equal one kalpa.

KIRTA - Devotional service.

LEELA - The divine play of the Self.

MAHATMA - Title of respect.

MAYA - Illusory world.

PUJA - Ritual of devotion.

SADHANA - Spiritual practice.

SADHU - Wandering ascetic.

SAHAJ SAMADHI - Natural absorption in emptiness while apparently engaged in the world.

SAMADHI - Absorption in bliss.

SAMSARA - The bondage of suffering on the wheel of incarnation.

SAMSKARAS - Past tendencies; impressions created by previous desires, thoughts, and actions.

SATSANG - Association with Truth [sat=truth, sang= community].

SATTVIC - Pure/clear.

SHAKTI - Divine energy.

SHANTI - Peace.

VASANAS - Latent tendencies, repressed subconscious identification.